Bible
Speaks
today

the message of

JOHN'S LETTERS

Series editors:
Alec Motyer (OT)
John Stott (NT)
Derek Tidball (Bible Themes)

the message of

JOHN'S LETTERS

Living in the love of God
Revised edition

David Jackman

INTER-VARSITY PRESS
36 Causton Street, London SW1P 4ST, England
Email: ivp@ivpbooks.com
Website: www.ivpbooks.com

First published 1988
Reprinted 1989, 1991
Second edition (with study guide) 1992
Reprinted 1994, 1996, 1998, 1999, 2000, 2005, 2006, 2009, 2011
This edition published 2021

British Library Cataloguing-in-Publication Data
A catalogue record for this book is available from the British Library

ISBN: 978–1–78974–246–6
eBook ISBN: 978–1–78359–080–3

Set in 9.5/13pt Karmina
Typeset in Great Britain by CRB Associates, Potterhanworth, Lincolnshire
Printed and bound in Great Britain by Ashford Colour Press Ltd, Gosport, Hampshire

Produced on paper from sustainable forests.

Inter-Varsity Press publishes Christian books that are true to the Bible and that communicate the gospel, develop discipleship and strengthen the church for its mission in the world.

IVP originated within the Inter-Varsity Fellowship, now the Universities and Colleges Christian Fellowship, a student movement connecting Christian Unions in universities and colleges throughout Great Britain, and a member movement of the International Fellowship of Evangelical Students. Website: www.uccf.org.uk. That historic association is maintained, and all senior IVP staff and committee members subscribe to the UCCF Basis of Faith.

*For Heather, whose light and love, in Christ,
are my constant encouragement.*

Contents

Bible Speaks today

GENERAL PREFACE

The Bible Speaks Today describes three series of expositions, based on the books of the Old and New Testaments, and on Bible themes that run through the whole of Scripture. Each series is characterized by a threefold ideal:

- to expound the biblical text with accuracy
- to relate it to contemporary life, and
- to be readable.

These books are, therefore, not 'commentaries', for the commentary seeks rather to elucidate the text than to apply it, and tends to be a work rather of reference than of literature. Nor, on the other hand, do they contain the kinds of 'sermons' that attempt to be contemporary and readable without taking Scripture seriously enough. The contributors to The Bible Speaks Today series are all united in their convictions that God still speaks through what he has spoken, and that nothing is more necessary for the life, health and growth of Christians than that they should hear what the Spirit is saying to them through his ancient – yet ever modern – Word.

ALEC MOTYER
JOHN STOTT
DEREK TIDBALL
Series editors

Author's preface

It was in the autumn of 1982 that I began the adventure of studying John's letters with the congregation of Above Bar Church, Southampton. On Sunday evenings, for over six months, we climbed the 'spiral staircase' of John's first letter and marvelled at his exposition of the things that matter most. There is a deceptive simplicity about John's style. So often the simplest vocabulary is combined with the most profound theology. Ideas that on the surface appear easy to grasp are shown on further investigation to possess ever-increasing depth, as themes interweave and new perspectives open out. After several years of living with John and trying to immerse myself in his message, I have sometimes felt defeated by the magnificence and complexity of it all. Yet, in other ways, I have constantly been encouraged to read the text again, to think it through again and to go on wrestling with the material. Isn't that one of the experiences that makes Bible study so exciting? 'He has . . . set eternity in the human heart; yet no one can fathom what God has done from beginning to end' (Eccl. 3:11). John's letters are certainly in that category.

In trying to share John's message with others, I have been particularly encouraged by the congregations who attended the Keswick Convention Holiday Week in 1983, and in fellowship with the Tenth Presbyterian Church, Philadelphia, USA, with whose Sunday morning congregation I was privileged to share 1 John over the summer Sundays in 1986, when I enjoyed a pulpit exchange with their pastor, James Montgomery Boice. These were wonderful weeks when as a family we experienced such a warm welcome and such a responsive hearing of God's Word. Truly for us it was a city of 'brotherly love'.

I studied and wrote over a period of five years. The final draft was completed during a period of sabbatical leave from Above Bar in the spring of 1986. I am most grateful to my secretary, Linda Burt, for her patient typing and retyping of the manuscript, to my colleagues on the staff team at Above Bar for their support, advice and encouragement, and also to the editorial staff of IVP for their gentle persistence and valuable editorial functions. It has been a privilege to contribute to the series and I would like to express my sincere thanks to John Stott for his original invitation (so long ago!), and for his patient understanding and generous encouragement to see the work through to completion. I have benefited also from other readers of the manuscript at different stages, who have made valuable suggestions for which I am most grateful.

It is one of the glories of the Bible that whenever you immerse yourself in a particular part, its contents seem to become the most important and urgent message in the world. I have no doubt that John's letters are a vital and powerful word from the Lord to the contemporary church situation around the world. In a day of polarization to extremes and consequent fragmentation of churches and individual lives, we need to heed his call to hold together truth and love on the basis of God's self-revelation throughout the Scriptures and especially in this text. It is my prayer that this exposition will help its readers to understand and apply unchanging truth, with genuine Christian love, to the multitude of perplexities, challenges and opportunities we face, as God's people, in our generation. We dare not be sidetracked by substitutes. 'Dear children, keep yourselves from idols.'

DAVID JACKMAN

Chief abbreviations

AV	The Authorized (King James) Version of the Bible, 1611.
Bruce	*The Epistles of John*, by F. F. Bruce (Pickering and Inglis, London, 1970).
Candlish	*A Commentary on 1 John*, by R. S. Candlish (1886), in the Geneva Series of Commentaries (Banner of Truth, 1973).
Clark	*First John: A Commentary*, by Gordon H. Clark (Presbyterian and Reformed Publishing Company, Phillipsburg, New Jersey, n.d.).
JBP	*The New Testament in Modern English*, by J. B. Phillips (Collins, 1958).
Lenski	*The Interpretation of 1 and 2 Epistles of Peter, the Three Epistles of John and the Epistle of Jude*, by R. C. H. Lenski (Augsburg, Minneapolis, 1966).
Marshall	*The Epistles of John*, by I. Howard Marshall, in the New International Commentary on the New Testament (Eerdmans, Grand Rapids, 1978).
NEB	The New English Bible (NT 1961, 2nd edition 1970; OT 1970).
NIV	The New International Version of the Bible (1973, 1978, 1984, 2011).
Plummer	*The Epistles of St John*, by A. Plummer, in the Cambridge Greek Testament for Schools and Colleges (Cambridge University Press, 1894).
RSV	The Revised Standard Version of the Bible (NT 1946, 2nd edition 1971; OT 1952).
RV	The Revised Version of the Bible (NT 1881; OT 1885).

Westcott   *The Epistles of St John: The Greek Text with Notes,*
            by B. F. Westcott (Macmillan, London, 1883; republished
            with Introduction by F. F. Bruce, Eerdmans, 1966).

Introduction

Jerome tells us that when the aged apostle John became so weak that he could no longer preach, he used to be carried into the congregation at Ephesus and content himself with a word of exhortation. 'Little children,' he would always say, 'love one another.' And when his hearers grew tired of this message and asked him why he so frequently repeated it, he responded, 'Because it is the Lord's command, and if this is all you do, it is enough.'[1] To any student of the letters of John, this story rings with authenticity. The NEB entitles the first letter 'Recall to Fundamentals', and that takes us both to the heart of the writer's concern and to his penetrating relevance to our contemporary situation. But before we can appreciate their message fully, or feel the force of their searching analysis in our own lives, we need to know a little about why these letters came to be written and who their author was.

1. The historical setting

It is very probable that the author of these letters was also the author of the Fourth Gospel and that he was the apostle John. There are so many parallels of thought and expression in these documents that few scholars have been prepared to follow the suggestion that more than one author was involved.[2] What we have before us in 1 John is a circular letter, though unaddressed, unsigned and without any of a letter's usual characteristics of style. It was probably sent from Ephesus to the congregations of Asia

---

[1] Jerome, *On Galatians* 6.10, quoted by Plummer, p. xxxv.
[2] Expounded by C. H. Dodd, *The Johannine Epistles* (The Moffatt New Testament Commentary, London, 1946).

Minor which were under John's special care, towards the end of the first century.

We know that after Christ's ascension John remained for some time at Jerusalem, as one of the 'pillars' of the church (Gal. 2:9). While Peter and James took the lead, Luke's careful account in Acts does not exclude references to John's involvement in the early days (e.g. Acts 3 – 4). He certainly seems to have been present at the Council of Jerusalem (Acts 15:22). Perhaps John remained in the city until the conflict of the years immediately preceding the destruction of the temple, the city and the Jewish nation by Titus in AD 70. Many believers, including the apostles, fled the city in those days just before the siege, in obedience to the command Christ had given (Mark 13:14) and it seems likely that John made Ephesus his new base. Irenaeus, a disciple of John's disciple Polycarp, tells us that the apostle continued in the church at Ephesus until the times of Trajan (AD 98–117).[3] Clearly the apostle lived to a great age. He would therefore have experienced exceptional authority as the only remaining apostolic link with the earthly ministry of the Lord Jesus, and these letters may well have been the last of the canonical Scriptures to be written, probably during the decade AD 85–95.

2. The moral climate

Why did John come to live in Ephesus? And how does his having done so affect the letters themselves? The destruction of Jerusalem follows quickly on the heels of the first fierce blasts of persecution under the Roman emperor Nero in the mid 60s, when Peter and perhaps Paul were martyred. As Christians fled from Jerusalem and from Rome, Ephesus – the greatest of all the Asian trade cities – became the natural centre for the growing churches. The church had been founded by Paul in about AD 55, and had probably been pastored by Timothy (1 Tim. 1:3). Doubtless it had grown in the intervening years, and its geographical location and importance made it a natural focus for the churches of Asia Minor. In the letters to the seven churches in Revelation, Ephesus is addressed first (Rev. 2:1–7).

That letter to Ephesus shows something of the pressures under which the church existed in a pagan city given over to idolatry and superstition. The huge religious industry, centred on the vast, magnificent temple of

---

[3] Irenaeus, *Against Heresies* 3.3.4.

Artemis (Diana), was a source of enormous material wealth – and of spiritual bankruptcy, characterized as it was by gross immorality and the bizarre rites of eastern pantheism (see Eph. 5:1–20). Clearly connected to this was the city's addiction to magic and sorcery, on which many of the founder members of the church had decisively turned their backs (Acts 19:19). It is not surprising, when we consider this background, that John's letters insist on right moral behaviour as the touchstone of a true Christian faith. Christians cannot continue to live in darkness (1 John 1:6), to love the world (2:15), to believe every spirit (4:1) or to have anything to do with idols (5:21). Love for the God who is light means a radical break with every kind of evil.

But it was out of this moral morass that the issues of false teaching and theology arose, which are the major concern of these letters and which we must now consider briefly.

3. The theological issues

Many of the New Testament letters were written primarily to correct false teaching and its resulting distorted behaviour, to combat heresy and immorality. In this the Johannine letters are no exception. What distinguishes them is their comparatively late date, which means that the opponents John is dealing with were more sophisticated and subtle in their presentation of error than some of their predecessors. Their system was still developing and it needed strong counteraction.

The first letter is directed to a specific situation in the churches, where false prophets have separated themselves and their followers from the main body of believers (2:19) and so divided the church. Their reasons for this action seem to have centred on their claim to a special 'anointing' (*chrisma*) of the Holy Spirit, by which they had been given true knowledge of God (2:20, 27). This knowledge (*gnōsis*) became the centre of their distinctive beliefs and lifestyle. Eventually these tendencies developed into a widespread and varied movement to which scholars have given the generic title 'Gnosticism'. John's concern, as we shall see, is to emphasize and define what is a true knowledge of God. 'We know' is one of his favourite, recurring assertions (see 2:3, 5; 3:14, 16, 19, 24; 4:13; 5:2; etc.).

One of the gnostic teachers active in Ephesus at this time was a man called Cerinthus. A Jew from Egypt, he sought to combine Old Testament ideas with gnostic philosophy, rejecting all of Paul's letters and accepting only parts of Matthew and Mark from the New Testament writings. This higher 'knowledge' did away with the characteristic Christian revelation, centred on the person of Jesus, under the guise of reinterpreting the message from a more advanced intellectual standpoint. It was actually a philosophy of life which had no foundation in the investigation of historical facts, such as the birth and resurrection of Christ. Rather it was imaginative, speculative, insisting that what may be thought is the ultimate test of reality. 'We may describe it as a series of imaginative speculations respecting the origin of the universe and its relation to the Supreme Being.'[4] Among the many strands of gnostic belief, we can note two major ones which are vital to our understanding of John's context. The first is the exaltation of the mind, and therefore of this speculative knowledge, over faith and behaviour. The second is the conviction that matter is essentially evil because the physical world is the product of an evil power.

How did this work out in the thinking of those infected by these gnostic teachings? First, they denied the incarnation of Christ (2:22; 4:2–3). It was a logical deduction from their belief that matter was evil. How could the supreme deity condescend to be united with an impure physical body, as a man? To get around the obvious historicity of Christ, men like Cerinthus seem to have propounded the theory known as Docetism (from *dokein*, to seem). According to this teaching the divine Word, the heavenly Christ, did not truly become man. He only *seemed* to have a human form, and there were those who maintained that Christ's body throughout his earthly life was a phantom. Others were prepared to admit the reality of the body of Jesus, but separated Jesus from the Christ. The earthly Jesus was born and suffered, but the Christ did not unite himself with Jesus until the baptism, and withdrew again before the passion and the cross. So not only was the person of Christ as truly human and truly divine under attack, but also the reality of his suffering and therefore its efficacy, not to mention the resurrection of the body. According to the Gnostics, redemption involves being set free from the pitiful state of being imprisoned in a body.

John is in no doubt about the nature of such teaching and teachers. Three times he describes them as 'liars' (2:4, 22; 4:20). He urges his readers

---

[4] Plummer, p. xxi.

to apply to every teaching they hear the test of the fundamental truths of the tradition they have already received, which has as its foundation the real incarnation of Christ. His true humanity is underlined by John's conviction that Jesus Christ the Son of God 'came by water and blood' (5:5–6) and that the blood of Jesus, the eternal Son, 'purifies us from all sin' (1:7). To the Gnostics, to describe the eternal Son as having flesh and blood was unthinkable; to John it was the heart of our salvation. His body given for us, his blood shed for us, was the atoning sacrifice for the sins of the world (2:2; 3:16) and the supreme demonstration and guarantee of the love of God for humanity (4:10).

False teaching always leads to false living, and the ethical implications of Gnosticism are equally John's concern throughout the letters. Here the claim of the false teachers was to have attained moral perfection through their superior enlightenment. They no longer sinned. Unlike some exponents of the gnostic creed, this does not seem to have led these teachers back into gross pagan immorality, but rather into an arrogant superiority which despised ordinary Christians, who remained ignorant, in the darkness. Such an attitude led them to separate themselves from the churches, as a new moral and spiritual elite. John's concern is to examine the nature of true light and darkness, and to link real spirituality with love for all other Christians in an unbreakable chain (4:20–21). His own affection for his readers is amply illustrated by his frequent reference to them as 'dear children' (*teknia*) in 2:12, 28; 3:7, 18; 4:4 and 5:21, and as 'dear friends' (or 'beloved'; *agapētoi*) in 2:7; 3:2, 21; 4:1, 7, 11. As Lenski comments, 'This is the voice of a father.'[5]

These letters therefore are dealing with matters of the utmost crucial importance for the churches. Gnostic teaching struck at the root of all Christian teaching, in both Old and New Testaments. It denied that God was the creator of the material universe, denying that it was 'very good' (Gen. 1:31) and claiming that it was essentially evil and inferior. This led the teachers to deny the reality of Christ's incarnation, atoning death and bodily resurrection, and with that to redefine sin and redirect Christian behaviour. It is not surprising that John recognized in such a frontal attack 'the spirit of the antichrist . . . already in the world' (4:3). For John this was not a local skirmish with one or two heretical individuals. The foundation principles of faith and conduct were being eroded and the young churches

---

[5] Lenski, p. 363.

were thrown into confusion. 'When the foundations are being destroyed, what can the righteous do?' (Ps. 11:3).

John has no doubt as to the answer. Doubtless aware of the special personal relationship he had had with the real, historical Jesus in his incarnation, John proceeds to state and reaffirm the great central truths of God's revelation in Christ, to give assurance that those who believe in the incarnate Son really do have eternal life. Just as his gospel was written so that we might believe (John 20:31), so John's first letter is written that believers may know that they have eternal life (5:13). The signs of reality and therefore the marks of assurance are not mystical and philosophical but down-to-earth and observable. To profess knowledge of God without a holy life, without a clean break with sin and a deep love for other Christians, is as much a delusion as to deny the incarnation of our Lord Jesus Christ. Belief and behaviour are inseparable. Mind and heart belong together. True light leads to real love.

Nearly two thousand years on, the need for John's teaching to be heard, received and applied is as great as ever it was. As the present century progresses all sorts of ingenious distortions of historic, orthodox biblical Christianity abound. Leading academics and church dignitaries are unwilling to affirm without hesitation the incarnation of Christ, or his sacrificial atoning death, or his bodily resurrection. Biblical morality is under attack within the church, as well as outside it, in such matters as sexual behaviour or the sanctity of human life. Scriptural marker posts which have guided generations are systematically removed in the name of a new hermeneutic or modern scholarship. We need to be recalled to the things that matter most, in our generation, as much as John's readers did.

We may laugh at the fantastic speculation of the Gnostics regarding the origins of the universe and their unscientific dualism, but is not the heresy of the supremacy of knowledge as alive as ever it was? Do we not need to learn from John that it is men and women's sinful rebellion against God, not their ignorance, that is our chief problem? Is it not still true 'that light without love is moral darkness'?[6] We are not lacking contemporary teachers who, while claiming to build on an apostolic foundation, want to take Christians on to 'deeper' truths beyond Scripture and to a fuller life. Adding to God's Word in Scripture has probably caused more heresy and division in the church than denying certain truths or subtracting from

---

[6] Plummer, p. xxix.

the Bible. 'The gospel and . . .' is at the root of many errors. John will help us to resist the fashion that sees the revelation of God in Scripture as dated and inadequate. This is the view which expresses itself in the formula, 'Go to the Bible for what God said yesterday, but to the prophet for what he is saying today.' The implied opposition between the two is in itself alarming. What Scripture said, it still says. And what Scripture says, God says. We need to take seriously what John teaches about those who claim to have received new revelation from God which can give a new vitality to a Christian's life and experience that the apostolic teaching never provided.

As we have seen, the errors of John's day were really an accommodation of Christian faith to the prevailing ideas of the secular culture. In every generation the church is challenged by the world, either to confront or to absorb its culture, to be 'squeezed . . . into its own mould', or to 'let God re-mould your minds from within' (Rom. 12:2, JBP). Today we are in danger of reflecting the existentialist philosophy of our society and not challenging it. That is why we Christians so often base our judgment and conduct on our personal feelings and experiences rather than on God's revealed truth. It is why we are conditioned by subjectivism rather than by the great objective realities of God and his Word. John does not attempt a detailed analysis or critique of error; he has no need to do so. He proclaims the truth in the characteristic apostolic confidence that where the truth is declared and believed, error will be undermined and will ultimately collapse.

4. The literary structure

Before we turn to the text we need to recognize the problems of analysing John's writing in a systematic way. Unlike Paul, John seldom argues a case, so it is difficult to trace a linear, logical progression of thought. The links between ideas are not always clear and the transition is usually very gradual. Lenski describes the first letter as 'built like an inverted pyramid or cone',[7] the base being laid in 1:1–4 and the whole letter being an 'upward broadening' of these themes. For myself, I have found the image of a spiral staircase the most helpful. As you climb the central staircase in a large palace or stately home, you see the same objects or paintings from a different angle, often with a new appreciation of their beauty. It is rather like

---

[7] Lenski, p. 366.

that with the great truths John is concerned to state and revisit in the letter. The view gets more wonderful as you climb and the heavenly light shines more and more clearly until you reach the top. Or perhaps one should think of a presentation of colour transparencies in which one magnificent photograph after another fills the screen, each dissolving into the one that follows it. How can you analyse such a presentation?

I have therefore decided to present the material section by section, recognizing, as all the commentators do, that the first letter takes as its foci the two great statements concerning the divine nature that God is light (1:5) and God is love (4:8, 16). In a general way these two affirmations correspond to John's concern about right believing and right behaviour, uniting for us, for all time, doctrine and experience, mind and heart, Word and Spirit, truth and love. If some formal grouping of the sections is required it may be that the following pattern will be helpful to others as it has been to me:

Walking in God's light (1:1 – 2:14),
Practising God's truth (2:15 – 3:10 and 4:1–6),
Living in God's love (3:11–24 and 4:7–21),
Sharing God's victory (5:1–21).

The second and third letters are of course easier to deal with, in that they are shorter and more specifically focused. Nevertheless, the themes of truth and love are strongly interwoven throughout them both, and we shall find much in them to underline and reinforce the lessons taught in the major letter.

1 John 1:1–4

1. The prologue

1. Foundation facts (1:1–2)

The opening of the letter, without any formal preliminaries, is as startling as it is difficult. In the original, the object is placed first and expanded by a number of clauses, until we eventually reach the main verb 'we proclaim' in verse 3. Because this is so difficult to understand, most modern English versions, like the NIV, anticipate the verb by inserting it in verse 1. Many divide up the long opening into more manageable units, as does the NEB with its arresting wording:

> It was there from the beginning; we have heard it; we have seen it with our own eyes; we looked upon it, and felt it with our own hands; and it is of this we tell. Our theme is the word of life.

Clearly to John the theme is more important than the telling; that is why he places it first for emphasis. But what is this *Word of life* which was there *from the beginning*? The phrase echoes the start of the Gospel of John ('In the beginning was the Word, and the Word was with God, and the Word was God') and beyond that the very first verse of the Bible in Genesis ('In the beginning God created the heavens and the earth'). Go back as far as you will in your imagination, says Genesis, before anything that exists came into being, and you will find God, the eternal Being. Go back to that same point, says John in his Gospel, and you will find Jesus Christ with God, because he was God, before anything was created. But the thought here is not quite the same, for it is not creation but the incarnation that is the focus of John's interest. And his concern in the letter is to declare that the Word which was made flesh in the womb of the virgin Mary was the same eternal Son of the Father who was before all time and who was the agent of all creation. The Word of life did not merely come into existence at Bethlehem; he already existed from the very beginning *with the Father* (2). This phrase (Greek, *pros ton patera*) indicates the closest sort of face-to-face fellowship, existing in the eternal mystery of the Godhead. It was this everlasting Word that became the human Jesus. There can be no separation between the two. It is true both that there never was a time when the Word was not and also that there was a definite moment of time when that Word of life *appeared* (2a), when it was manifested and experienced by human beings in this material world of time and space.

But this interpretation raises a difficulty. We have said that the *Word of life* is to be equated with the earthly Jesus. But John begins the letter with four neuter pronouns (*ho*) – *that which . . . which . . . which . . . which*. These cannot stand in opposition to the masculine noun translated *Word* (*logos*). If the *logos* is really Christ himself it would seem strange to refer to him as 'that which' rather than 'he who'. Does John therefore mean something other than the historical masculine person of Jesus when he uses the term *logos*? It can have a wider meaning, of course; it can refer to the Christian message, or gospel, the revelation of God in holy Scripture. Thus, when Paul exhorts Timothy to 'preach the Word' (2 Tim. 4:2) he clearly means the whole counsel of God, not just the person of Christ. Some Christians talk about 'getting into the Word' when they are describing their study of the Bible. Some have suggested that 'the message [*logos*] of the gospel' (see Acts 15:7) is what John is proclaiming rather than the historical person of the incarnate Son.

Certainly the grammar leads us in that direction, but the verbs in verse 1 also demand our careful consideration. Undoubtedly a message can be *heard* and even *seen*, but *looked at* and *touched* are stranger verbs to use of an impersonal Word. The word for *looked at* 'expresses the calm, intent, continuous contemplation of an object which remains before the spectator'.[1] But *touched* with *our hands* together with *seen with our eyes* emphasizes the personal encounter and objective experience of a true revelation. Could John ever forget the invitation of the risen Lord to his bewildered, frightened disciples, who were convinced they were seeing a ghost? 'Touch me and see; a ghost does not have flesh and bones, as you

---

[1] Westcott, p. 6.

see I have' (Luke 24:39). Both 'touch' and 'see' can be used in a non-physical sense to mean mental contemplation or intellectual testing, but neither is the natural meaning in this context.

Perhaps the key to the problem lies in the precise meaning of the phrase the *Word of life* – which is also a wonderful truth. Clearly John's emphasis here is on *life*. This is what he develops in verse 2, and indeed *the Word* is not mentioned again after this in the letter. It seems best, then, to understand the genitive *of life* as being in apposition to *the Word*, which would give the meaning 'the Word which is the life'. And what is that word or message if it is not Christ himself? This theme runs throughout John's writings. Jesus himself asserted, 'I am . . . the life' (John 11:25; 14:6) and taught that the Father has granted the Son to have life in himself (John 5:26). 'In him was life, and that life was the light of all mankind' (John 1:4). The life is the divine nature itself, in all its powerful, external personhood and dynamic activity.

> Paul could say, 'We preach Christ' (1 Cor. 1:23; cf. 2 Cor. 4:5) showing that the message and the person are ultimately identical . . . Our writer here wants to emphasize that the Christian message is identical with Jesus; it took personal form in a person who could be heard, seen and even touched.[2]

How does this relate to the difficulty of the neuter pronouns? The neuter conveys more than the masculine alone would do. The historical Jesus is the Christ of faith. The gospel in which we believe and by which we are saved is the eternal Son of the Father who 'for us men and for our salvation came down from heaven; by the power of the Holy Spirit he became incarnate of the Virgin Mary, and was made man'.[3] Christ *is* the gospel. The person and the message must be held together.

When we consider all this against the background of the church situation explored in the introduction, we can begin to see how every clause of this complex introduction has its own edge and significance. Verse 2 makes this especially clear. *The life appeared; we have seen it and testify to it.* Here is the authentic apostolic witness to the reality of Christ's identity as the eternal Son, seen in his earthly life, guaranteed by their personal experience.

---

[2] Marshall, p. 102. See footnote for a fuller discussion and documentation.

[3] Nicene Creed (*Alternative Service Book*, Rite A).

This is why we can have confidence in their testimony. Although we have not seen, the apostles did. The evidence in the person of Jesus convinced them of the reality of the gospel and thrust them out to proclaim it. The eternal life John refers to was *with the Father*, so he is not talking about the new birth which is the experience of all who trust in Christ, but the life of the Eternal which always was. It is this divine life which has been manifested in human history, in a real man, who really lived, really died and really rose again from the grave; in Jesus of Nazareth. John and his fellow apostles heard him speak. They saw him with their own eyes; not as a mystical vision, but in living reality. It was more than a momentary glimpse; rather, it was a consistent daily revelation. They touched him physically both before his death and after his resurrection. This was no spirit being, disguised in a temporary human suit of clothes. Neither was he a mere man on whom 'the Christ' descended for a period of time. He who was from the beginning and whom John heard and saw and physically touched was the Word who is the life.

Jesus, the man, was also nothing less than God. Cerinthus and his followers might theorize from their imaginative, philosophical base; but they were not witnesses. They had not seen or heard or touched. Only by dismissing the true witnesses were they able to maintain their destructive heresies. Only by making John into a liar could they deny that this earth is indeed 'the visited planet'.[4]

2. Everyday experience (1:3–4)

As we study John's letters, we shall see over and over again how he relates doctrinal truth to daily life, by weaving the two strands together into one cord of Christian orthodoxy. He is not alone among the New Testament authors in insisting on the marriage of learning and living. It is of course an implicit criticism of the false teachers, who exalted 'knowledge' to the highest place, and a rebuke to much contemporary evangelicalism, which divorces a correct theology from a Christlike life. It is sadly all too possible to know the truth without doing it, to profess the faith without expressing it in a consistent life. Some of the strongest rebukes and warnings of the New Testament are reserved for such double-mindedness, which is, at

---

[4] C. S. Lewis.

root, hypocrisy. James warns us against self-deception (Jas 1:22–25), and Jesus identifies such an attitude as evildoing (Matt. 7:23).

Having come at last to the main verb *we proclaim* in verse 3, we see that John's concern in the remaining part of this prologue is to point out the practical application of the apostolic testimony to the lives of his readers. The order is vitally important to grasp. The message proclaimed is the person and work of Christ, the incarnate Son of God. He is both the source and the substance of the eternal life which John wants his readers to know they have. That life is now defined in terms of a fellowship, or relationship, with the Father and the Son. This is itself in keeping with the words of Jesus recorded by John in his Gospel as part of the Lord's high-priestly prayer: 'This is eternal life: that they know you, the only true God, and Jesus Christ, whom you have sent' (John 17:3). Believing God's truth brings us into a living union with God – fellowship with the Father and the Son. That is the fellowship the apostles knew and enjoyed, but it is something which every believer can share with them. Our blessings are none the less real because they rest on faith rather than sight. As Jesus told Thomas: 'Because you have seen me, you have believed; blessed are those who have not seen and yet have believed' (John 20:29). Faith is the door to fellowship.

The word *fellowship* (*koinōnia*) is an interesting one. Used in classical Greek as a favourite expression for the marriage relationship, the most intimate bond between human beings, it is particularly appropriate to describe the Christian's personal relationship with God and with fellow believers as here, and later in verses 6 and 7. But the word also meant a participation or sharing in a more general sense – for instance, a business partnership or a joint tenancy. Perhaps John could look back on the distant days when he and his brother James had been shareholders in the Zebedee Fishing Company. Their relationship to their father and so to each other, within the family, gave them a common concern. This will prove to be one of the letter's great thrusts. There is no other way into genuine membership of the body of Christ, into true fellowship with God, than by believing the apostolic testimony. You cannot know God without knowing Christ. You cannot know fellowship without receiving the truth.

All true spiritual unity is therefore grounded in the gospel. That is the treasure which all believers have in common, in these 'jars of clay' (2 Cor. 4:7). Because we have Christ and he has brought us to the Father, we all belong to the one family. We all have the same privilege as the apostles to address him in the most intimate personal terms, to use the family's name, 'Abba' – dear Father. And because we belong to him, we belong to one another. 'We are family; we are one.' Without that fellowship with the Father there can be no lasting earthly unity. That is why all attempts to cobble together a unity of human origin between groups of professing Christians on any foundation other than God's revealed truth in Scripture, the Word of life that is the gospel, are bound to fail. Fundamental gospel unity already exists between those whose fellowship is with the Father and the Son. We do well to pray and work for its increasing manifestation and activity in a time of such confusion and perplexity as this.

In our desire for visible unity among Christians, however, we must not forget that it is fellowship with God that comes first; fellowship with one another is derived from it. Tradition cannot provide a basis on its own for a true church unity, nor can a common experience, which is a notoriously subjective standard. The truth of the Scriptures is the only adequate foundation for fellowship. The basis of all lasting *koinōnia* must be the theological realities of what God has done in and through his Son, Jesus Christ, which John is about to reaffirm in this letter.

Before he does so, let us note that other practical stimulus to maintaining a living fellowship with God – a *joy* that is constantly increasing (4). There is some discussion as to whether the text should read 'our joy' or 'your joy' (the Greek manuscripts differ), though the former is more likely and seems to be best supported. But both are true, since we may surely enjoy the latter in our own experience. Later John will write, 'I have no greater joy than to hear that my children are walking in the truth' (3 John 4). But what greater joy could there be for his children too? The conscious possession of eternal life, the daily enrichment of personal fellowship with the living God, the deepening awareness of oneness with all God's people everywhere – could there be any comparable recipe for fullness of joy? Such joy is quite different from human happiness. As a spiritual song of a bygone generation put it, 'Happiness happens; but joy abides.'[5] Three times in the upper room, in the face of the cross, Jesus spoke of the joy that awaited his disciples (John 16:20, 22, 24), joy that would be complete and indestructible. But it came to them only through the cross and because he gave himself resolutely to fulfil his Father's purposes (see Heb. 12:2–3).

---

[5] CSSM chorus, 'I'm Happy When Everything Happens to Please'.

Let us never forget that the realities to which John testified, and in which our faith is grounded, include the death of our Saviour on the cross, which opens up our pathway to joy. To the extent that we are convinced of the total sufficiency and efficacy of that sacrificial death, we shall know a deep joy which no-one can drain, a full joy which nothing can quench. And we shall share something of John's heart as we realize that nothing is more enriching or more wonderful than helping others to that same conviction too, and seeing their fellowship deepen.

1 John 1:5–7

2. Walking in God's light

'If God made men and women in his own image,' it is said, 'then we have returned the compliment.' That is the root of most of our problems. All sin is in essence an attack upon the character of God. We are not willing to believe that the living God really is as the Scriptures reveal him to us. We have a vested interest in resisting the claims of the 'transcendental interferer', as C. S. Lewis once called God. So we reject God's revelation and construct a substitute more in accordance with our likes and needs. This is the heart of human rebellion; we will not let God be God in our own lives. We would rather have our idols. We are like the character in one of G. B. Shaw's plays, whom the playwright describes as 'a self-made man who worships his creator'. You see the symptoms every time someone says, 'But I like to think of God as . . .' Usually what follows is a picture of a benevolent, avuncular figure whose main purpose is to satisfy the whims of his creatures, or some other distortion of the God revealed to us in the Scriptures.

But if our view of God is distorted, everything else is bound to be out of joint. Perhaps it is for this reason that John begins the letter proper by launching us into one of the greatest theological statements of the whole Bible, *God is light* (5). There is much that he needs to correct in both the doctrine and the morals of the churches to which he was writing, but he begins not with their eccentricities, but with God. Not for nothing did the Greek church call John 'the theologian'. While the whole Scripture record from Genesis to Revelation shows us God's attributes, revealed in his words and his actions, John alone seeks to expound the essence of the nature of God, in the form of propositions which use the simplest language to convey the most profound concepts. It is John who records for us in the Gospel the teaching of Jesus to the Samaritan woman that 'God is spirit' (John 4:24). And in this first letter he adds that God is light and God is love (4:8). Light and love are his very essence, just as 'spirit' is. They describe not his characteristics, but his very being.

It is important to note how carefully John introduces this first key statement, which will dominate the first half of this letter. The revelation that *God is light* is not a discovery which John has made as a result of his philosophical explorations, but a message he has received. It was heard *from him*, a clear reference to Jesus Christ, last mentioned at the end of verse 3. As always, the apostolic task was to announce to others what they had heard from the Lord. The church's task similarly is to keep this 'pattern of sound teaching', to 'guard the good deposit that was entrusted to you' (2 Tim. 1:13–14), and to do this by entrusting it to 'reliable people who will also be qualified to teach others' (2 Tim. 2:2). So there is an unbroken chain of witnesses to the truth of God as revealed in Christ and to the apostles from the beginning down to the present day. We are no more at liberty to redefine or 'modernize' the message than they were. God's revealed truth is not negotiable. So John stresses the divine source of what he is about to declare. The authority for his teaching lies in what he has heard in the historical revelation of God, in Jesus Christ.

John's authority to write and our authority to believe rest on the crucial importance of this disclosure of the hidden eternal life of God, in time and space, in Jesus of Nazareth. What more authority could anyone want, or need? Against this, his opponents could offer only their own speculative fantasies.

1. The content of the message (1:5)

God is light; in him there is no darkness at all. The positive is characteristically reinforced by an equally strong negative which might be translated absolutely literally 'and darkness, in him, no, not any at all!' The two are utterly incompatible. What does light suggest to us? Minds taught by Scripture go back to Genesis 1:3: 'And God said, "Let there be light," and there was light.' Here is the earliest expression of the nature and will of the Creator. His words execute his purposes; both words and actions together reveal his character. The God who creates begins with light, as the primary expression of his own eternal being. And from this everything else grows. Without that light there would be no plant or animal life; no growth, no activity, no beauty would be possible. All creation owes not only its existence, but its sustenance, to the God who is light, and the Christ who declared himself to be the light of the world (John 8:12; Col. 1:16–17). Not surprisingly, light became a frequent symbol of God's presence in the Old Testament, finding one of its clearest expressions in the exodus, when Israel experienced that 'the LORD went ahead of them in a pillar of cloud to guide them on their way and by night in a pillar of fire to give them light, so that they could travel by day or night' (Exod. 13:21). This function, as a source of illumination and guidance, probably lies behind John's emphasis here on walking in the light as an essential of Christian discipleship.

The other major significance of God as light in Scripture is as a picture of his perfect moral righteousness, his flawless holiness. John's thought here is paralleled by Paul's assertion in 1 Timothy 6:16 that God 'lives in unapproachable light'. His 'otherness' is demonstrated by the prophet Habakkuk's conviction, 'Your eyes are too pure to look on evil; you cannot tolerate wrongdoing' (Hab. 1:13). A foundation stone of right Christian believing and living, then, is that intellectually, morally and spiritually *God is light*, unsullied and undiluted. It speaks of holiness and purity, of truth and integrity; but also of illumination and guidance, warmth and comfort. As Faber has so beautifully expressed it:

> My God, how wonderful thou art,
> Thy majesty how bright,
> How beautiful thy mercy-seat,
> In depths of burning light!

> How wonderful, how beautiful
> The sight of thee must be,
> Thine endless wisdom, boundless power,
> And aweful purity![1]

Such light scatters all our darkness. It is the truth against which all other claims must be tested. For it is the nature of light to penetrate everywhere unless it is deliberately shut out. The light reveals the reality,

---

[1] Frederick William Faber (1814–63).

and while it dispels darkness, it also exposes what the darkness would hide. The point is well made in one of C. S. Lewis's insights when he comments that we believe the sun has risen not because we see it, but because by it we see everything else. There are no twilight zones in God. If we interpret this verse theologically, John is saying, 'God is truth and error can have no place with him'; if ethically, he is saying, 'God is good and evil can have no place beside him.'[2]

We are now in a position to see the personal implications of claiming to be in relationship with such a God. Clearly there can be no higher human privilege than to have 'fellowship . . . with the Father and with his Son, Jesus Christ' (3). That is why John is writing the letter and that is why we are given life, for 'the chief end of man is to glorify God, and to enjoy him for ever'.[3] But it makes a nonsense of this possibility to imagine that we can live some sort of compromise existence, with one foot as it were walking in the light with God, and the other remaining in the darkness of the world. One of the first lessons of messing about in boats is that it is impossible to exist for long with one foot in the boat and the other on the river bank. The spiritual 'splits' are equally impossible! To illustrate this, John now proceeds to examine and demolish three false claims which were current in his day and which are still prevalent in our own. The first of these will occupy our attention for the rest of this section.

2. The claim that sin does not matter (1:6–7)

Each of the wrong attitudes, or false claims, with which John now deals is prefaced by the same introductory phrase, *If we claim* . . . (see 6, 8 and 10). Using the touchstone of reality that God is light, we are now provided with three marks of the reality of the claim to be in fellowship with this God, or three tests which can be applied to prove whether or not such a claim is genuine.

In verse 6, the mark of unreality is to say that we have fellowship with God, while actually living a life marked by unrighteousness. The idea of 'walking' indicates a persistent movement in a particular direction, what we might call a 'lifestyle'. The proof of verbal claims to be orthodox in our beliefs and truly to know God is a holy life, and for that there can be no

---

[2] Marshall, p. 109.
[3] Westminster Shorter Catechism.

substitute. A person who persists in sin cannot be in touch with God. The two states are mutually exclusive. You might just as well live in a coal pit and claim that you are developing a suntan! Put that way, we may well ask how anyone could ever make such a claim. What did John really have in mind?

There are two things to note. The positive correction which follows in verse 7 emphasizes *fellowship with one another* (between Christians) as evidence of walking in the light. This implies that the darkness John is especially concerned about in verse 6 is the attitude that imagines, 'I can have fellowship with God without fellowship with my fellow believers.' This particularly applied to the false teachers who were dividing their followers from other Christians by claiming a superior knowledge and experience. John's point is that their attitude to others negates their claim to be walking in the light. The second point, which leads from this, is that those who walk in the darkness but claim to be in the light are actually redefining sin. The false teachers did not regard their unwillingness to value and love other Christians as sin. They minimized and excused it; indeed, they positively justified it, as the grounds of their extra 'insights'. Nevertheless, as John is to teach several times in the course of this letter (2:9, 11; 3:11–14; 4:20–21), no-one can truly love God without loving his children (5:1).

Moreover, to redefine sin and to fail to be convicted of it as sin in our lives is a certain indication that we are not walking in the light. A true Christian will find the searchlight of God's truth constantly exposing the parts of life that need to be confessed as sin and left behind, through the life-changing power of the Holy Spirit. Walking in the light means living each day with God who *is* light. The nearer I come to God, the more conscious I shall be of my own sin and rebellion. So the greatest saints have always been conscious of themselves as the worst of sinners (1 Tim. 1:15). Christians who live in God's light do not find it difficult to walk together in fellowship. The light shows the way ahead, and enables them to coordinate their actions and move forward in harmony. Where Christians are at variance, or separate from one another, it is always true that someone is already walking out of fellowship with Christ. This does not mean that we shall all agree about everything, but that is not the essence of fellowship anyway. It is about loving one another and valuing one another, so that we can agree to differ without severing the ties that bind us to one another as sons and daughters of the light.

One further thought at the end of verse 7 is that as the light of God reveals our sin, we shall keep appropriating the cleansing that comes through Christ's death, by our own repentance and faith. Notice that the present tense, *purifies*, denotes continuous action. 'Keeps on purifying' would be an equally good translation. Frequently we Christians are deprived of the enjoyment of walking in the light because we feel we have failed so often, perhaps in a recurring or besetting sin, that we dare not come back to God to ask for fresh forgiveness. We cannot say, as it were, 'Lord, it's me again and it's that again.' This is to fall for the devil's lie. There is a glorious inclusiveness about this present tense and its application to *all sin*. We can never come too often to God when we come in humble penitence and active faith. It is because this blood (7) is that of God's Son that it has such virtue. Its purifying properties extend to each and every sin. To walk in the light means to become increasingly conscious of sin that would hinder our fellowship with God and our fellow Christians, and as that sin is revealed, not to run away into the darkness again. Rather we bring it, by faith, to the God whose Son gave his life that all our sins might be forgiven and removed. As we do so, the barriers to fellowship are removed and we continue in that relationship with God.

Sin does matter. We dare not redefine it, or pretend it doesn't exist. If it demanded the price of the blood of God's only Son on the cross then it is of paramount importance that we take it seriously, accepting God's definition of where and what we are by nature and receiving his abundant pardon and restoring love, by grace. This is the outcome:

Light has come into the world, but people loved darkness instead of light because their deeds were evil. Everyone who does evil hates the light, and will not come into the light for fear that their deeds will be exposed. But whoever lives by the truth comes into the light, so that it may be seen plainly that what they have done has been done in the sight of God. (John 3:19–21)

21

1 John 1:8–10

3. Radical treatment for sin

To claim to be in a personal relationship with God, but to walk out of his light, in disobedience to his command, is empty nonsense. His commands are in themselves the expression of his character. This groundless pretence to a real relationship with God was the first of the false claims which John had to expose. But although the contradiction might seem self-evident to us in its spiritual logic, apparently there were those who denied the charge in spite of their false teaching and twisted morality. This is because the second and third false claims stem from the first, and are both equally dead ends.

    a. 'I'm not a sinner' – the denial of the sinful nature (8).
    b. 'I haven't sinned' – the denial of sinful actions (10).

1. Two dead ends (1:8, 10)

a. Denial of the sinful nature (1:8)

The claim to be sinless is in itself an evidence that we are not walking in fellowship with God (*the truth is not in us*). 'This doesn't mean simply that they are telling a lie, but that they have no share in the divine reality despite their claims to the contrary.'[1] Walking with God in the light means that our lives are continually being searched by his truth so that we begin to realize how many marks of sin we have within us.

---

[1] Marshall, p. 113.

At one time the walls of my sitting room were painted white, and in ordinary or artificial light they looked fine. But on occasion I used a wall to act as a screen for showing colour transparencies. What a difference the intense light of the projector bulb made! Every imperfection and mark was shown up for what it really was. God's light is like that. It shines in the Scriptures and we see how far short of God's standards we fall, how far we have strayed from the pathway, how frequently we have transgressed his commandments. Its shines supremely in Jesus, the light of the world, whose perfect life shows us our own shabby, grubby lives by comparison. Walking in the light is not always a comfortable experience. As we walk in it, we become more conscious of our sin, not less.

This explains why comparatively new Christians can sometimes become discouraged. Many times I have had to counsel those who have become depressed only a matter of months or a year or so into their Christian experience. This is because, as they often put it, 'I seem to be more of a sinner than ever I was before.' But notice what is happening. Their sense of sin is a result of walking in the light! They are seeing actions, words or attitudes as sin now which had never been sin to them before. Their consciences are being educated and sensitized by the Spirit through God's Word. One of God's projects in the life of every growing Christian is to peel back more and more layers of our hidden depravity and sinfulness (as we can bear it), so that we start to see ourselves as we really are, in God's sight. This project has the glorious end purpose that we should become clean deep down. Our danger is that we resist this process of conviction and cleansing, that we buck and bridle, or that we allow God to go so far and then no further. It is worth considering how we find ourselves reacting when God's light exposes some specific sin in our lives. It is too easy to dodge the issue, to look for the first escape route, excusing it as 'one of my little weaknesses'. That is the way into darkness.

But the subtlety of this denial of our sinful nature is that it can appear in the most seemingly spiritual clothing. Down the centuries there have been groups in the church who have believed and taught that it is possible for a Christian to live *without sin*. By this they do not mean simply enjoying the victory of faith through union with Christ, which Romans 6 teaches. Rather they believe that the old sinful nature is so subdued as to be eradicated and as a consequence they teach that life can be lived on a totally higher plane. The introduction of such teaching can appear to have excellent motives. There is a desire to magnify the work of Christ in his atoning death and dynamic resurrection, and to exalt the power of the Holy Spirit in the Christian, overcoming the down-drag of sin within us. Often a specific experience is advocated ('full surrender', a 'second blessing', 'brokenness', a 'release of the Spirit') as a means by which sin can be dealt with once and for all. Such teaching, in fact, is a snare to some very sincere, spiritually minded Christians who long to be more like Christ, and who would love to be lifted beyond sin and temptation. But John tells us that if we think that we are without sin, we are deluded. We *deceive ourselves* – but probably no-one else, and certainly not God. He at least knows the truth about us (Heb. 4:13). Others too may see much more clearly than we do how weak and failing we are. A self-deluded person is the saddest of all. We can all conjure up pictures of angry people, turning purple and about to let off a head of steam as they grimly protest through their teeth, 'I am *not* losing my temper!' It is a dead end to deny that I am a sinner by nature; though I must never allow that confession to lull me into thinking that I can continue in sin, as we shall see later in chapter 3 of John's first letter (3:6, 9).

Because this danger and its close cousins are so widespread today, it may prove valuable to pause a moment longer to examine its roots. Commentators on the Synoptic Gospels have frequently pointed out that in his ministry, Jesus proclaimed both the fact that the kingdom of God was now present, and also that it had not yet come in its fullness. That completion awaits the 'last day'. The Old Testament looked forward to the Day of the Lord when God would establish his reign in the world. Naturally the Jews saw this as a single day. But Jesus taught that the kingdom already in their midst in the person of the King and the lives of his followers (Mark 10:14; Luke 17:20–21) awaits its fulfilment in the age to come (Luke 19:11ff.). As G. E. Ladd puts it,

> The church lives 'between the times'; the old age goes on but the powers of the new age have irrupted into the old age . . . There is a two-fold dualism in the New Testament: God's will is done in heaven; his Kingdom brings it to earth. In the Age to Come, heaven descends to earth and lifts historical existence to a new level of redeemed life (Rev. 21:2–3).[2]

---

[2] *A Theology of the New Testament* (Lutterworth, Guildford and London, 1975), p. 69.

Failure to realize that this is true in every dimension of our experience of the kingdom has led to the errors and unrealistic claims we are dealing with here.

In the physical realm, it is sometimes claimed that there is total healing in the atonement. This is not the place to embark upon a discussion of the complex question of healing. But it seems to me that we shall receive total healing only when death itself is defeated and we are in our resurrection bodies (1 Cor. 15:35ff.). Meanwhile we can thank God that he does continue to heal in this world, according to his sovereign will, with or without medical means. But even Lazarus, raised from the dead by the Saviour himself, died again. Perfection waits for heaven. Only then will our weaknesses and deformities be removed. And so it is in the spiritual realm. The power of the indwelling Christ can give us increasing victory over sin in this life, but we do not have heaven on earth. We shall carry our sinful nature with us every day until we die or Christ returns. 'When Christ appears, we shall be like him, for we shall see him as he is' (3:2). In his presence we shall be on the seeing side. Now we live by faith, not by sight (2 Cor. 5:7).

Let us leave this issue with an incident recounted about Charles Haddon Spurgeon, the great Baptist preacher of the nineteenth century. Perhaps few other Christians in heaven will have such a long queue of preachers apologizing for having told so many apocryphal stories about them! Be that as it may, it is said that Spurgeon was once confronted by a man who claimed to be 'without sin'. Intrigued, the preacher invited him home to dinner. After hearing the claims through, he picked up his glass of water and threw it in the man's face. Understandably, the visitor was highly indignant and expressed himself very forcefully to the preacher about his lack of courtesy. To which the wise man replied, 'Ah, you see, the old man within you is not dead. He had simply fainted and could be revived with a glass of water!'

b. Denial of sinful actions (1:10)

In a sense, this is the darkest of the three false claims. The quick succession in which they follow one another introduces us to a typical feature of John's writing, as we realize that what might at first sight seem to be reflection, or even repetition, is in fact building and developing his thesis. The difference in wording between verse 8 and verse 10 is therefore significant. Here in verse 10 we move from the inward principle of the sinful nature to the outward symptoms that confirm the existence of the disease – the outward actions of sin which show what we are like inside. To deny these is the grossest kind of darkness. Yet it happens all the time in our culture, and it infects our church life too. We no longer call sin 'sin'. Adultery becomes 'having an affair'. Theft is 'helping myself to the perks'. Selfishness is 'standing up for my rights'. The last thing we human beings will admit is that we sin.

For over a century now, optimistic evolutionary humanism has convinced generations that there is nothing fundamentally wrong with human nature in general, or with you and me in particular. And that is in face of the reality of recent history! John is in no doubt as to what this means, whether it surfaces in the world or in the church. It indicates that humanity is in the darkness, that there is no real dependence on Christ at all. To deny this central biblical truth of the universal sinfulness of humanity is to accuse God of libelling humanity and misleading the whole human race. It could not be more evident that God's revelation in Christ has never found a home in our lives (10b). We must not be surprised when the chickens hatched by atheistic philosophies come home to roost, in terms of multiplying lawlessness and a society which will prove increasingly difficult to govern. But we must resist that drift with all our energy, in our own lives, in our churches and in our community.

In order to have any meaningful concept of sin we must accept that moral standards exist, that some actions are always right and others always wrong. But the only way in which such moral absolutes can be justified is by reference to a creator God, who has determined the structures of reality. If God is dead, everything is permitted. But God's righteous character remains absolute in his world, and deviation from that character, as revealed in God's law, remains sin. That law is not an arbitrary set of rules designed to restrict and inhibit human life, but the expression of God's will for human relationships in accordance with his own nature of light and love. That is why adultery, theft, lying, murder and all the other sins remain sin, whatever people may call them. The other sins include those commonly tolerated among Christians too – the favourite sins of greed, jealousy, envy, malice, bitterness and a critical or unforgiving spirit. They are all equally attacks on the character of God to whom we are all finally responsible. Before him, we all stand guilty. If we deny that these things are sin, we are actually calling God a liar. That is meant to shock us. We deny his Word. We say his revelation is not true. We embrace the darkness. If one has never seen oneself as a guilty sinner before a holy God and desperately in need of his forgiveness, then one cannot yet be a Christian. There can be no fellowship with the God who is light.

2. God's way through (1:9)

What an amazing verse this is, and what a wonderful way forward! The answer to denial is confession. For confession recognizes that a particular action or course of behaviour is morally wrong and goes on to admit that we are personally guilty of that wrong. That is doing the truth. It demonstrates a positive response to God's light. It is important here to notice the plural, *sins*, which implies a detailed and specific confession of our wrong thoughts, words, actions and attitudes. It includes the good which we omit, as well as the evil which we do. It is comparatively easy to admit that we are sinners, in a general sort of way, much as people will say, 'Well, no-one is perfect.' That might meet the false claim of verse 8, but not of verse 10. If we are to continue in fellowship with God we must be prepared to let him deal radically with our lives. We shall have to come often to admit, 'Lord, *that* was sin. I recognize it was wrong and I confess that I am guilty. I ask for your forgiveness and the power of your Spirit to keep me from its repetition.' Confession of that sort is of course really repentance. It is identifying what is wrong (sin) and who is responsible (us) and asking God in his mercy and grace to deal with both, through the work of Christ.

This verse seems to assume that the confession will be directly to God, not to a priest or to a fellow Christian. There is indeed a place for confessing our sins to one another, as mentioned in James 5:16. The context there, however, seems to imply that this will be where some illness has been caused through a breach in human relationships. If we have offended someone, then it is our responsibility to go to him or her, admit our sin and guilt, do anything we can to make reparation, and ask for forgiveness. That person can (indeed must, as a Christian) extend forgiveness in so far as we have offended, but he or she cannot of course forgive us in an absolute sense for our sin against God, in causing that offence. But there must be forgiveness if a right relationship is to be restored, whether between human beings, or between a human being and God. Incidentally, that is why the commonly held view that all we need to do is to apologize is quite inadequate. Is that all we need to do to God? Indeed not. A mere apology can be as much an expression of remorse as of repentance. As verse 9 teaches us, a true confession of sin asks for and anticipates forgiveness. This is not on the grounds of the intensity of our repentance, but on the grounds of what Christ did when he died for our sins on the cross. But if this is how we are to approach God, can we imagine that simply apologizing can rebuild fellowship with another Christian? Forgiveness must be asked for, given and received, for fellowship in the light to be totally restored.

The rest of this wonderful verse shows us how God responds to such requests, and the two strands beautifully balance the false claims we have been examining.

a. *He is faithful and just* – the confirmation of the divine nature.
b. *He . . . will forgive . . . and purify us* – the confirmation of the divine actions.

a. Confirmation of the divine nature

These two assurances about God's character are the ground of our own assurances about forgiveness. He is *faithful* to his own nature, for it is impossible for him to act in any other way than is consistent with his moral perfection. 'If we are faithless, he remains faithful, for he cannot disown himself' (2 Tim. 2:13). Therefore he is faithful to his Word, which is the expression of his own nature. He keeps the promises which he has made, and none who put their trust in him will be disappointed or rejected. So when God promises to forgive all those who truly repent and put their faith in Christ, we can rely on him to keep his word. This was the foundation confidence of all the apostolic preaching.

But, equally, God is *just*. We must not water this down into meaning 'kind' or 'merciful'. Rather it expresses his inflexible righteousness. But this too guarantees our forgiveness. God's justice ensures that he will give to all people their due. Were it not for the sacrificial death of Christ, we would tremble at that thought, for the justice of God would rightly condemn us for our sin and cast us into outer darkness. But as chapter 2 will teach us, we have a Saviour who has turned away God's wrath, who has died in our place and whose blood goes on cleansing us from sin. Having lived the perfect life that we have failed to live, he died the death that we deserve to die. The fact that the penalty for our sin was paid by Jesus means that God will not demand a second payment. In Christ the work is accomplished, once and for all, and we are forgiven. The justice of God requires him to forgive, because the debt has been met. What we deserve is God's judgment, but this is just what he does not give us. Instead, we receive what we do not deserve, and that is his mercy and pardoning grace. These great truths have become a favourite theme in Christian praise, but perhaps they have rarely been so simply and yet profoundly expressed as by Charitie Lees Bancroft:

> When Satan tempts me to despair,
> And tells me of the guilt within,
> Upward I look, and see him there
> Who made an end of all my sin.
>
> Because the sinless Saviour died,
> My sinful soul is counted free;
> For God, the just, is satisfied
> To look on him and pardon me.[3]

b. Confirmation of the divine actions

God forgives and he purifies. Forgiveness absolves us from the punishment of sin which we deserve. Purifying frees us from its pollution. We have seen how the mercy and justice of God join at the cross to produce a free, eternal forgiveness as the outcome. Every one of our sins can be covered by the death of Christ. But the light of God wants to deal with our darkness. That is why it has been manifested. So the backward look to forgiveness covering our past, whatever it may have been, is now balanced by the forward look to the holiness, the cleanness which must increasingly characterize our future. 'The one affects peace, the other our character.'[4] For the same cross that pardons, promises power to live differently. As our old self is crucified with Christ, the way is opened for us to share in the newness of his resurrection life. This salvation offers the possibility of becoming increasingly like the God whose fellowship we are learning daily to enjoy.

The two parts of the divine action answer to the two aspects of righteousness already noticed. As judging righteously God forgives

---

[3] 'Before the Throne of God Above', by Charitie Lees Bancroft (1841–1923).
[4] Plummer, p. 30.

those who stand in a just relation to Himself: as being righteous He communicates His nature to those who are united with Him in His Son.[5]

This is God's glorious way through our dead ends. Our part is to ensure that we travel with him.

---

[5] Westcott, p. 25.

1 John 2:1–6

4. Marks of Christian reality

God is light. His perfect righteousness is totally consistent and nothing can alter the truth of his character. On this basis, which undergirds all other forms of truth, John continues to test the claims of those who affirm that they know God and live in his light. After all, if a person claims to be living in fellowship with God, that should be verifiable by the sort of life he or she lives in the world. Inconsistency here explains why so many have written off Christian belief as an irrelevant fiction. How can these 'Christians', who claim to know God, be so unlike him? Nothing is a greater stumbling block to the agnostic. The biggest hindrance to the spread of the Christian message has often been within the Christian church itself.

This does not mean that anything short of perfection in our Christian lives denies the truth of the gospel. We have already learned that no Christian can claim to be without sin in this life. That sort of perfection waits for heaven. But we have a goal which defines our present direction, and for all of us much more progress towards that goal is always possible. It is the direction in which our life is travelling which determines whether or not our Christian profession is genuine.

For example, in a course of academic study we have to begin with the elementary principles and master those before the more demanding levels can be attempted. Any student quickly comes to recognize that all the possibilities of the chosen discipline cannot be exhausted, but as the student learns and matures he or she is moving in that direction. Soon the student discovers that those who are the authorities in that subject are even more aware of how much they do not know, so that the greatest scholars are frequently the humblest of people. On the journey to

31

knowledge and experience the student will often stumble and blunder, trying to learn from mistakes, and above all pressing on. There is an instructive parallel in this to the life and experience of a real Christian. Perhaps John Newton, the converted slave-trading sea captain who became a minister of the gospel, expressed it most helpfully when he said, 'I am not what I ought to be; but I am not what I once was. And it is by the grace of God that I am what I am.'

In these verses, John highlights three characteristics of that sort of biblical reality. Christians know who Christ is, trust what he did, and do what he commands.

1. Christians know who Christ is (2:1)

When John Wesley left home, his mother, Susannah, is said to have written these words in the flyleaf of the Bible he was given: 'Sin will keep you from this book, but this book will keep you from sin.' The apostle John knew the power of God's Word to defend his people from the attacks of the enemy and to inspire them to holy living. That is one reason why he writes to them. Like the psalmist, every Christian needs to be able to say, 'I have hidden your word in my heart that I might not sin against you' (Ps. 119:11). But knowing his *dear children*, and being the realist he is, John also knows that there will be occasions of defeat in every Christian's life. So the mark of reality is not a hazardous 'perfection', which is only obtainable by redefining sin. Rather, it is seen in what we do about the sin 'that so easily entangles' (Heb. 12:1). That depends on our having a genuine knowledge of Christ, what he has done and what he is doing for us. Our belief about Christ is always the foundational test for reality in scriptural experience. If we are wrong here, nothing else will be right.

He is *Jesus*, his earthly name which anchors him in history as a real man, not a figment of anyone's imagination. But it also introduces us to the purpose of his earthly work. 'Give him the name Jesus, because he will save his people from their sins' (Matt. 1:21). He is *Christ*, the anointed one, the Messiah. We know from the Gospels that he was concerned to expand the inadequate understanding of his contemporaries beyond the limited ideas of Messiah as a warlike conqueror or a nationalistic superhero. The heart of the messianic secret lay in his claim to be not only David's son, but David's Lord (Mark 12:35–37). This implies 'that Jesus is supernatural in dignity and origin and that his sonship is no mere matter of human descent'.[1] It was for this reason that he was crucified. Indeed, his identity as 'Christ' is so central to the early church's understanding of Jesus that *Christos* was used virtually as a proper name. Born at Bethlehem, as a human child, he was nevertheless pre-existent with the Father. He is the Son of God.

Bringing the two natures of Christ together, like a golden thread running through both, is the fact that he is *the Righteous One*. As to his eternal deity, he is righteous by definition, because he is God. As to his earthly life, he is also righteous, in contrast to sinful humanity. His life was sinless, though he endured temptations far beyond anything we are called to face: he simply never yielded to them (Heb. 4:15).

It is this which enables him to be *an advocate with the Father*. The person of Christ leads us on to his work. The Greek word is *paraklētos*, meaning originally one who is called alongside to help someone else. So it came to have the general meaning 'advocate'. John describes the Holy Spirit by the same title in the Gospel (14:16, 26; 15:26; 16:7). The fact that Jesus describes the Spirit in John 14:16 as 'another advocate' (*allos paraklētos*), implying 'another of the same kind', indicates that he accepted both the title and the role as properly describing himself.

This dual means by which Christ's righteous life enables him to be our advocate is also brought out by Peter. 'For Christ also suffered once for sins, the righteous for the unrighteous, to bring you to God' (1 Pet. 3:18). It is because his sinless life was laid down for us as the means by which our forgiveness was obtained that he can righteously plead his sacrifice before the righteous Father, on behalf of us, the unrighteous.

A true Christian does not make false claims about perfection, but neither does he or she become careless and blasé about behaviour, as though sin did not matter. Instead, the true Christian recognizes, with gratitude, that committing sin does not make the Christian life hopeless. The very presence of Jesus Christ, the Righteous One, before his Father is enough to guarantee forgiveness and secure restoration.

2. Christians trust what Christ did (2:2)

Here the key word is *atoning sacrifice*, or in some translations 'propitiation' (AV, RV) or 'expiation' (RSV). The thought is that the substance of the

---

[1] Vincent Taylor, *Mark* (Macmillan, London, 2nd edition 1966), ad loc.

case presented for our defence by our advocate is that he himself is the sacrifice that atones for our guilt. There has been considerable disagreement between translators and commentators as to which translation is to be preferred, but the basic concept is not difficult to grasp. The word *hilasmos* is used on only one other occasion in the New Testament, and that is in this very letter, in 4:10.

In the Septuagint (the third-century BC translation of the Old Testament into Greek), at Ezekiel 44:27, the term is used to translate the Hebrew word for 'sin offering': 'On the day he goes into the inner court of the sanctuary to minister in the sanctuary, he [the priest] is to offer a sin offering for himself, declares the Sovereign LORD.' This is helpful in explaining the central idea for us. The priest, a sinful human being, was to offer a sacrifice to enable him to enter the presence of the righteous God. This helps us to see that the Lord Jesus offered himself on the cross as the means by which punishment is changed to forgiveness and wrath to mercy.

The advantage of the translation 'propitiation' is that it includes the idea of turning away the wrath of God from the sinner to the substitute. This concept has been widely criticized as unworthy of the God of the Bible, and caricatured as reducing him to the level of a pagan deity who has to be bribed to be gracious. But such criticism disputes or rejects the fact that the Bible reveals a God whose attributes include wrath and justice, however unpleasant or inconvenient human beings may find that to be. Even if we omitted all the Old Testament references to God's wrath, of which there are many, we would still find many in the New Testament. 'Whoever rejects the Son will not see life, for God's wrath remains on them' (John 3:36). 'The wrath of God is being revealed from heaven against all the godlessness and wickedness of people, who suppress the truth by their wickedness' (Rom. 1:18). 'Because of these [i.e. whatever belongs to your earthly nature], the wrath of God is coming' (Col. 3:6). As Gordon H. Clark comments,

> All sorts of rituals can be called atoning sacrifices. But salvation, in the Christian sense of the term, requires one very definite type of sacrifice, namely a propitiation . . . John is perfectly specific. Christ's atoning sacrifice is a propitiation. Its aim was to appease the wrath of an angry God; and it succeeded in doing so.[2]

---

[2] Clark, p. 46.

Christians rejoice because in his mercy and grace God has provided the means by which sinful people like us can be justly forgiven and welcomed into his presence, sure that we are accepted by him, that God no longer has anything against us. That means was the death of his Son. At the cross, Christ paid the penalty demanded by God's broken law, that was due from us. In paying it to the full, he both upheld the righteousness of God and met the deepest need of human beings. 'Love and faithfulness meet together; righteousness and peace kiss each other' (Ps. 85:10). God's justice and his mercy are equally satisfied. Because we are made in God's image there is a sense in which we human beings instinctively know it has to be this way. We do not want an amoral universe in which there is no retribution for the likes of Hitler. Constantly we cry out for justice. But what we desperately need ourselves is mercy. Only that can keep us from being consumed by the fire of God's holiness (Lam. 3:22; Heb. 12:29). His wrath is neither an emotion nor a petulant fit of temper, but the settled conviction of righteousness in action to destroy both sin and the sinner. The glory of the gospel is that we have an advocate who pleads for mercy on the ground of his own righteous action when he died the death that we deserve to die. Once the penalty has been paid, there cannot be any further demand for the sinner to be punished. God has himself met our debt. He came in person to do so. The cross is not the Father punishing an innocent third party, the Son, for our sins. It is God taking to himself, in the person of the Son, all the punishment that his wrath justly demands, quenching its sword, satisfying its penalty and thus atoning for our sins.

And not only for ours but also for the sins of the whole world. Does this mean that Christ has propitiated God by expiating the sins of every human being who has lived or will live? If so, it must follow that all enmity between humanity and God has been removed. There are many who would want to claim such a meaning for these words and go on to proclaim a salvation which is universal, irrespective of whether or not an individual believes in Christ, or even hears of him. Evangelism then becomes merely the announcement of what God has done, and in which all will automatically share. If this was really what John meant, the letter would be flawed by a glaring contradiction. What then of the 'antichrists' who 'went out from us, but . . . did not really belong to us' (2:19)? Are they automatically forgiven and restored? The letter would lose much of its purpose if that were so. What are we to make of the assertion in 3:10 that some are 'children of the devil'? 'Anyone who does not do what is right is not God's

child, nor is anyone who does not love their brother and sister.' How are
we to cope with the bald statement 'There is a sin that leads to death'
(5:16)? If we assume that John is not contradicting himself, we must ask
ourselves what he does mean by *the whole world*.

The fact that John distinguishes here between 'us' (the church) and *the
world* means that he is using *the world* in his most characteristic way, to
indicate those who are at present outside of Christ. At other times John
uses the word (Greek, *kosmos*) to mean the earth, or the human race, but
most frequently it carries the connotation of the world in rebellion, the
mass of unbelievers, who reject Christ's claims. This is the world for which
Christ died. Every Christian was once a part of it. 'Nor will John let his
readers think of their blessings in restrictive terms. The propitiation that
has availed to wipe out their sins is sufficient to do the same for all.'[3]
(Actually, the words *sins of* are added by the translators, though they are
perfectly in keeping with John's designation of Jesus, in the Gospel, as 'the
Lamb of God, who takes away the sin of the world'; John 1:29). As we share
the good news with others we can have confidence that Christ's sacrifice
is indeed as the Prayer Book describes it, 'a full, perfect and sufficient
sacrifice, oblation and satisfaction, for the sins of the whole world'.[4]
No-one need be excluded.

This is surely the meaning of the event in the temple, described in
Matthew 27:51 as happening at the moment of Christ's death. The thick
veil, or curtain, which separated the worshipper from the holiest place of
all, which only the high priest was allowed to enter once a year on the Day
of Atonement, was torn in two, from top to bottom, by the hand of God,
not by a human hand. It is as though God was saying to the whole world
of sinners, 'You may come in now.'

3. Christians do what Christ commands (2:3–6)

Verse 3 introduces us to a phrase which is to recur several times in this
letter: *we know*, or 'by this we may be sure' (RSV). The third mark of spiritual reality is that we obey Christ, that he is our Lord in deed and not
simply in theory. Jesus himself told his disciples, 'If you love me, keep my
commands' (John 14:15). As with many other of his statements, this is not

---

[3] Bruce, p. 50.
[4] Order for Holy Communion, Book of Common Prayer (1662).

a popular view today, even among some who would want to be called Christians. The fact that to talk about obedience to God's Word is often parodied as 'legalism' is symptomatic of a false dichotomy between law and love. Not long ago a young Christian told me that he no longer needed to obey Christ's Word (or even read it) because 'I just love him.' By contrast, Jesus said, 'If you keep my commands, you will remain in my love, just as I have kept my Father's commands and remain in his love' (John 15:10). Grace does not abolish God's law; it internalizes it, by writing it on our hearts. That is why 1 John 2:4 reinforces the preceding verse, by denying its opposite. The disobedient person who professes to be a Christian is a liar (Greek, *pseustēs*), because such claims are blatantly contradicted by behaviour. How can the truth of God be in such a person?

'Actions speak louder than words,' we say. We mean that they are a closer indication of the real person, a better window into the soul. Words are comparatively cheap. They can easily deceive. Whatever he or she may claim, the person who disobeys God does not actually and truly know God *as* God. To do so would be to bow unquestioningly to God's authority, wisdom and power. That person would say, 'God knows best and that is the way I want to go.' In fact, every time we refuse to obey God, we accept the slander against his character which lies at the root of all temptation. We are saying that we know better than God, and that simply means that we do not actually know God well enough. For truly to know God is to love him. And truly to love him is to obey him. There can be no substitute for this. We need to be on our guard against self-deception in this, because we can all so easily be deluded, especially if we are relying on the subjective evidence of our feelings rather than the objective truth of God's Word. The young couple who told me that they were living together, although unmarried, because they had prayed about it and felt God was saying it was all right for them were flatly contradicting the fact that God had already said in Scripture that it was *not* all right. Either they did not know God's character or they did not love him enough to obey him.

This is the link with verse 5. Once again John swings to the opposite pole, but as always with each swing he adds a little more to what he is saying. The more we obey God's Word, the more we open the door for his love to accomplish his purpose in our lives. The test of living in the light is growing in love for God. And the ultimate proof of that is not in the heightened emotion of exciting worship (though that may well be an expression of reality) but in the daily, detailed, disciplined obedience by which our characters are being transformed into the image of the God we love. Nor is that *word* simply one of imperative command, for wherever commands occur in Scripture they are surrounded by promises, which lead us to a deeper awareness of God's love for us and a deeper reciprocation in our love for him, as we trust and obey. The *complete* love of which verse 5 speaks is simply meant to underline for us the fact that obedience is the way to growth and maturity. 'John is here speaking, as often in this Epistle, of an *ideal* state of things. No Christian's love to God is perfect; but the more perfect his knowledge, the more perfect his obedience and his love.'[5]

The section ends with a renewed emphasis on our practical 'walk' (rsv) in everyday life. How did Jesus walk? Certainly in the light with God, due to his perfect obedience to the heavenly Father's will, to which God himself testified (Matt. 3:17; 12:18; 17:5). But he also walked in love towards the crowds of needy, lost people whom he daily encountered (Matt. 9:36). Walking in the light is characterized not only by the absence of sin but, equally importantly, by the presence of love. Those who remain (abide) in Christ cannot fail to display the fruit of the Spirit, in a Christlike character. Just as the life flowing through the vine enables the branches to bear fruit, and that fruit indicates the nature of the plant's life within, so it is with a true Christian who abides in Christ (see John 15:1–8). 'By their fruit you will recognise them. Do people pick grapes from thorn-bushes, or figs from thistles?' (Matt. 7:16). If we really walk in the light with God, our behaviour will become more and more like that of the Lord Jesus. It is not that we obey God's commands in order to make ourselves good enough to walk in the light with him. That is the cul-de-sac called legalism. Rather, those who truly walk with God love to obey him, because in that way they grow a little more like him each day. That is the high road called grace.

---

5 Plummer, pp. 38–39.

1 John 2:7–14

5. How the true light shines

With these verses John concludes the evidence by which we can know we are truly walking in the light with God. Real fellowship with God is marked by increasing consciousness and confession of sin (1:6–10), and by growing likeness in character to Christ through obedience (2:1–6). Now the emphasis comes to rest on the other mark of real fellowship with God, and a great theme of this letter: genuine love for fellow Christians.

1. The light shines in God's law (2:7–8)

The law is itself an expression of the love of God for human beings. Once we can grasp that, it will help us to see it in a much more positive way. A father used to ask his wife to go and see what the children were doing and tell them to stop. It is a slander against God's character to imagine that he is like that. The law of God does not inhibit; it enables. In our Western cultures we tend to give 'law' the impersonal inflexible connotation of the Roman *lex*. But the *torah* of the Old Testament is not an abstract code. It is the personal loving instruction of our omniscient Father, telling his children how to live their lives for maximum fulfilment. From the beginning of God's revelation the law of love was taught, because the law was an expression of the character and will of its giver, who is love. The levitical *torah* enjoined God's people to 'love your neighbour as yourself' (Lev. 19:18). When John speaks of *an old* command, *which you have had since the beginning,* he is probably meaning that this same instruction was among the first that they were given at the start of their Christian lives, and that we never outgrow it.

Jesus himself taught that the Law and the Prophets were all summed up in the law to love God and one's neighbour (Matt. 22:37–40). The apostle Paul echoed that 'the entire law is fulfilled in keeping this one command: "Love your neighbour as yourself"' (Gal. 5:14). So when John comes to the same conclusion, he knows that he is saying nothing new. There is nothing very novel about that sort of self-giving love; it is basic. It explains why he addresses his own readers as *dear friends*, more literally 'loved ones'. Love is basic.

Yet Jesus did call it a *new* commandment (John 13:34), and John seems to be remembering that in verse 8a. Perhaps the 'newness' relates to the fact that *its truth is seen in him*. For the only time in the history of the world that that command was lived out was in the human life of Jesus Christ, with a depth and reality no-one would otherwise have ever glimpsed or imagined. Though the command was old it was never out of date, and in Christ it was both renewed and fulfilled in the most complete way possible.

But the real surprise comes in the next words, *and in you*. That is staggering. We may wonderingly accept that the command to love was seen to be fulfilled in Jesus – but in *us*? Yes, that is what genuine Christianity, according to John, is all about. For with the coming of Christ the new age has dawned, with its new covenant, in which God puts his laws in our minds and writes them on our hearts (Heb. 8:10, quoting Jer. 31:33). The Christ who perfectly fulfilled that law has made available to us his divine resources of power to live that way also. As he was its embodiment and therefore our example, so we are to receive and reflect that *light*, as members of the new kingdom (8b). Already *the darkness is passing* away, and that process will continue, until eventually, with the completion of God's purposes, the darkness will be eradicated and perfect light will rule.

This is at once a great stimulus and encouragement to all God's children to live as children of the light.[1] This light is *true* in the sense of being genuine and therefore perfect, or complete. By contrast the light of the Law and the Prophets was at best imperfect, a shadow of the reality; and the so-called light of the gnostic teachers was in fact darkness. Only in Christ is the law of God perfectly fulfilled, and in that light, which still shines on in the darkness, we see what it means to be truly human and truly Christian.

---

[1] See in addition Paul's exhortations in Rom. 13:12–14; Eph. 5:1–2, 8–11; 1 Thess. 5:5–8.

2. The light shines in Christians' love (2:9–11)

Again the emphasis is on love, not knowledge. Anyone may claim to be in the light, or to know God, and it is easy to mistake intellectual understanding for spiritual reality. But true spirituality must infallibly express itself in love. Our natural reaction to John's use of the strong verb *hates* is to say that we cannot be guilty of such an extreme. But John would hardly have written the sentence if it were not a trap into which professing Christians might easily fall. Looked at from another angle, if our fellow Christians stand to us in a relationship of brothers and sisters, it is impossible for us to be indifferent towards them. As we have been learning about the brilliant white light which is the nature of God, we are not to resort in our own lives to what we may fondly imagine can be preserved as twilight zones, areas in which we can tolerate any lack of love towards our fellow Christians. If we are thankful to God for the way in which he has shone his light into our lives, how can we but be thankful for every one of our fellow Christians, who has had a similar experience of grace? We must determine to do everything we can to channel more of God's love into their lives by our active love towards them.

It is the positive activity of outgoing love to which John is encouraging us in verse 10. There is a certain sort of Christian piety which imagines that security is to be found by being hermetically sealed off from other people, even from other Christians, in a recluse-like detachment. In this way individuals are safe from the infection of those who may not believe as strongly or purely as they imagine they do; their edge is not blunted, their soundness is unsullied. Churches, as well as individuals, can be affected by this mentality. But it is not loving my brother or sister, who also seeks to walk in the light and who needs my fellowship. The more Christians get wrapped up in themselves, concentrating on the cultivation of their own character, or the preservation of their own virtue, the less clearly will they see the light. They have become self-centred and it will not be long before self-love takes over. And the greatest enemy of real love is self-love. That is the root of hatred. What Robert S. Candlish said over a century ago remains true: 'A selfish religionist is sure to become either morbid or stupid. It is by sympathy and brotherhood that the fire of personal Christianity is fanned.'[2] The absence of that positive active love for

---

[2] Candlish, p. 142.

others can be as sure an indication of walking *around in the darkness* as the more outward forms of hatred and violence. Those who live *in the light*, loving their fellow Christians, find no 'stumbling block' (*skandalon*) hidden in their pathway. This Greek word originally meant a bait-stick or a trap. The idea is of hidden danger which may ensnare and destroy the unwary, especially if they are travelling in the dark. The only remedy is to keep walking in the light.

Light and love go together. If we love people, we take care to avoid sinning against them, or causing them to stumble. We want to encourage them and build them up. But lack of love distorts our perspective and blinds our vision. We begin to feel at home in the darkness. We become used to groping our way through life, constantly stumbling and being ensnared by all kinds of problems. Such people are often unaware of how dark it is and how short-sighted they have become. Animals such as pit ponies, which are kept underground, eventually lose their sight. The light that is ignored soon ceases to strike us. The conscience that is habitually silenced soon ceases to speak. If we lack love, we are in the darkness.

3. The light shines in Christians' convictions (2:12–14)

The fact that the NIV prints these verses in the form of poetry illustrates that this section of the letter is a break point at which John looks back on the instruction he has already given before moving into a more detailed set of warnings against the world and the false teachers. It is perhaps an opportunity for the readers to assess the practical application of these truths to their own life situation. The structure is clearly and deliberately symmetrical. Verses 12 and 13 address, in turn, *dear children, fathers* and *young men* with the verb *I am writing*. Verse 14 follows the same order with the same three categories. (There are small stylistic variations in the Greek, but they do not affect the structure or meaning.)

But who are the *dear children*? Some commentators have seen in these verses encouragement to three age groups in the church,[3] though suggesting that this may refer to spiritual maturity rather than chronological age. However, because *dear children* is John's favourite phrase for addressing the whole congregation in the letter, it seems to me preferable

---

[3] Bruce, pp. 57–58.

to take the *dear children* to mean every reader. Remember that this letter comes from the pen of a revered and elderly apostle. *Fathers* would then mean the older church members, perhaps particularly the elders in whose hands the government of the church lay, while *young men* would signify the next generation. In neither case should we allow the masculine terminology to obscure the application of what John says to the women and girls of the congregation as well.

If we remember too that John has been dealing with the marks of real membership of the family of God, we shall see that the *because* clauses particularly highlight the convictions John wants each group within the churches to hold, since by these the light of God will truly shine in their lives. All children of God, therefore, should know that their *sins have been forgiven on account of his name* (12a) and that they *know the Father* (14a). They have those convictions about forgiveness and about fellowship which have been the substance of much of John's teaching so far. He is writing because of those convictions; not so much to declare them as to apply them and to underline the consequences which must follow a true enjoyment of them.

We can be God's dear children only because our sins have been forgiven, and that has happened *on account of his name*. As always in the Bible, the name indicates the nature. In contrast with Semitic usage, our names in English can be labels without any necessary content of meaning, but that is never the case in Scripture. Today, London Road may indeed lead to London if you follow it carefully enough for long enough, but Paradise Square is certainly no more than a label! When John talks about the name of Jesus, however, he is talking about his nature revealed by that name as saviour, rescuer. This was a dominant note in the earliest apostolic preaching. On the day of Pentecost Peter declared, 'Repent and be baptised, every one of you, in the name of Jesus Christ for the forgiveness of your sins' (Acts 2:38). A little later, explaining the miracle by which a lame man at the temple gate was healed, he informs the crowd, 'By faith in the name of Jesus, this man whom you see and know was made strong' (Acts 3:16). Again, defending the same miracle before the Sanhedrin, Peter states, 'Salvation is found in no one else, for there is no other name under heaven given to mankind by which we must be saved' (Acts 4:12). It is this forgiveness which brings us into a true knowledge of God, in the form of a personal faith relationship with him. All God's children know their Father and know that he has accepted them, in Christ.

The mark of maturity (*fathers*) is seen as a deepening of that knowledge. Twice John says he writes to them *because you know him who is from the beginning* (13a and 14b). This description of Christ takes us back to the opening verse of the letter and the prologue to the Gospel as it underlines the pre-existence and eternal deity of the Lord Jesus Christ. Ever since these leaders of the churches first responded to the gospel they have known that Jesus is God and that this is what enables him to accomplish the work of salvation (see 4:14). Their continuance in the light depends upon holding firm to their knowledge that Jesus is nothing less than God, whatever the false teachers may claim. When their churches are told that Jesus is the human son of Joseph, that the Spirit of Christ came upon him at his baptism and left him before his passion, and that therefore his blood is not that of the Son of God, the 'fathers' know better. They are to hold firm to the Word made flesh through whom all things were made, by whom all things hold together, who is the only light of humanity. There is no route to Christian maturity other than a deepening knowledge of Christ, and those who know him love him.

For the *young men* John identifies other priorities. They *have overcome the evil one* (13b). They *are strong, and the word of God lives in* them (14c). Here the emphasis is on victory over Satan which characterizes the beginning of real Christian experience and discipleship. To know that we have been rescued from the devil's grip, and that he has no more power over us, is part of the glorious assurance that God wants to give to even his newest children.

Verse 14 adds the further explanation that the real strength they enjoy as they walk in the light and battle for the truth is not simply that of their own natural youthfulness, but that supplied by the Word of God. 'Even youths grow tired and weary, and young men stumble and fall; but those who hope in the LORD will renew their strength' (Isa. 40:30–31). We develop that hope by listening to his voice. We derive our strength to fight and conquer the world, the flesh and the devil, from the truth of God's revelation in Scripture. It is indeed the sword of the Spirit (Eph. 6:17; Heb. 4:12). How important it is, then, that 'fathers' in the church should teach the 'young men' the Word of God. Nothing matters more for the future health and strength of Christ's body. The ultimate weapon against the gnostic errors was this letter and others like it in the New Testament, Scripture inspired by the Holy Spirit being in itself God's infallible revelation.

That is still our only guide in all we believe and in all our behaviour. Yet how many churches and Christian groups today are neglecting the teaching ministry? They will have no defence against the erroneous teachings which still seek to infiltrate Christ's church. They cannot be strong; they will not conquer. Such Christians will be borne away from their moorings by the prevailing currents. They may find themselves in darkness, rather than light. We need to share and hold these biblical convictions with integrity and enthusiasm if we are to remain true to our calling. This is how the true light shines.

1 John 2:15–17

6. What's wrong with the world?

If we are going to walk in the light with the God who is perfect holiness, we cannot sit loosely to sin in our own lives. We have already begun to realize that being a Christian calls for a thoroughgoing dedication to the will of God. We must actively enter into all that Jesus has made available to us through his death. We shall show the reality of our faith by obedience to God's will in every part of our lives. This in turn will strengthen and develop the reality of fellowship with him. Now John makes this same point in a different context, as he shows us that if we are going to love God, we cannot also love *the world*. The two are mutually exclusive as objects of our love.

We must begin by asking what John means by *the world*. After all the same Greek word (*kosmos*) is used by John in his Gospel, where he tells us that 'God so loved the world that he gave his one and only Son, that whoever believes in him shall not perish but have eternal life' (John 3:16). Are we not to be like God in demonstrating that sort of compassion? Yet later in this letter we shall find John telling us that 'the whole world is under the control of the evil one' (5:19). It is no wonder that Christians have had very differing attitudes towards the world. Sometimes in the history of the church the emphasis has been upon withdrawal from contact with the world, while at other times the church has been so enmeshed in the world that it has been difficult to see how Christians differed in their lifestyle from the secular society around them.

The fact is that the word *kosmos* has different shades of meaning in Scripture. Sometimes it stands for the natural world which God has created – Planet Earth. This is much the same meaning as in Psalm 24:1, 'The earth is the LORD's, and everything in it, the world, and all who live in it', although the word *kosmos* is not actually used here in the Septuagint. The natural world, created and sustained by God, expresses his character in its beauty and splendour. In this creation, humanity has a special responsibility to fulfil the divine mandate to 'rule over' all the earth, and over all the creatures (Gen. 1:26). So the 'world' comes to mean the whole human race, who are both the apex of the created order and, at the same time, God's vice-regents. This is the world that God loves enough to send his Son to rescue (John 3:16).

But there is another meaning of *the world* in the New Testament. Sometimes the world is seen as an organized system of human civilization and activity which is opposed to God and alienated from him. It represents everything that prevents human beings from loving, and therefore obeying, their creator. This meaning of *kosmos* has much the same content as John's term 'darkness' in chapter 1. The contrast between light and darkness could hardly be more stark. For John this is developed in a series of contrasts, such as truth and falsehood, love and hate, love of the Father and love of the world. That is why verse 15 is such a direct command: *Do not love the world.* James reminds us that 'friendship with the world means enmity against God' (Jas 4:4). Our contemporary danger is that we tend to water down this radical demand. We think that we can love the world a little bit. After all, 'What's wrong with it?' The world glitters and sparkles and draws us towards it; and many Christians, as well as those who are seeking Christ, have discovered that the alternative can look so unattractive, stodgy and old-fashioned. Too often the community of Christians can repel those who are genuinely open to Christ because it does not adequately reflect his vitality and love. No wonder people ask, 'If I do become a committed Christian, isn't that going to be very restrictive and inhibiting?' The church can look like a black and white photograph from a bygone age in comparison with the world's multicolour video presentation. And that problem is not new in the twenty-first century. John wants us to look to Christ and see that he is the one whom we are to be like, for only in him can we find our real freedom. It will help us to understand this if we can grasp what is involved in 'loving the world'.

1. The world: a deceptive attraction

In verse 16 John defines more clearly for us what he means by *everything in the world*. It is obvious that he is not thinking about 'things' in themselves, such as money or possessions, which are morally neutral. Rather he is talking about our personal attitudes towards these things. The 'worldly' characteristics of which the verse speaks are in fact reactions going on inside us, as we contemplate the environment outside. That is very true to Scripture's teaching concerning the fundamental roots of our problems. You could put human beings in the most perfect, favourable and natural environment and they will spoil and defile it. The reason is not because of deficiencies in the environment but because of what is going on inside them. As the Lord Jesus put it,

> What comes out of a person is what defiles them. For it is from within, out of a person's heart, that evil thoughts come – sexual immorality, theft, murder, adultery, greed, malice, deceit, lewdness, envy, slander, arrogance and folly. All these evils come from inside and defile a person. (Mark 7:20–23)

Small wonder that Mark Twain said that a man or woman is the only animal with the capacity to blush, and the only one that needs to! It is important that we grasp this perspective, since Christians have often been content to define 'worldliness' as consisting primarily in the things that people do or the places they visit. But John is concerned to show us that the world affects us much more deeply than that. The motives and attitudes of our minds and wills are what ultimately dictate our actions. Our affections are set either on this world or on God. It is impossible to love them both.

A striking biblical illustration of this is the account in Genesis 3 of the stages by which Adam and Eve fell from their original innocence into sin. Into a perfect environment the tempter came with his insinuating questions, which were really an attack upon the character of God. 'Did God really say, "You must not eat from any tree in the garden?"' (1). Did God really mean it? 'You will not certainly die' (4). Do you really have to believe it? 'For God knows that when you eat from it your eyes will be opened' (5). Each of these questions contains a suggestion that God is not to be trusted. His word cannot be depended on. He may change his mind. He's a spoilsport, whose only interest is to frustrate and inhibit you. So the original temptation was to break out of the straitjacket, to start 'living'.

And that is how the world still attracts us. It is a deceptive attraction, because if we insist on living independently of the God who made us, we shall find ourselves unable to fulfil the chief role for which we were created – that of knowing God personally. You may imagine that your goldfish swimming around in its bowl is tired of the straitjacket of its environment. You may even feel you should liberate it to the wider world of the living-room carpet! But that sort of freedom is freedom only to die. In the same way, men and women alienated from God are dead to those spiritual realities without which they cannot be completely human. But the devil will not let us believe that. Instead he uses the natural appetites, which God has created, in order to ensnare us.

> When the woman saw that the fruit of the tree was good for food and pleasing to the eye, and also desirable for gaining wisdom, she took some and ate it. She also gave some to her husband, who was with her, and he ate it.
>
> (Gen. 3:6)

There were three stages by which Eve was brought to succumb. The fruit satisfied her appetite for good food. She liked the look of it. She wanted it to make her a more fulfilled person, to boost her ego. It was as she and Adam disobeyed God that the human race fell into sin. So, in exactly the same way, John highlights three elements in the temptation of the world which the devil still uses to lure us away from the liberty of loving God with all our heart, soul, mind and strength. This is how the deceptive attraction still works on us.

First, John mentions *the lust of the flesh* – all that panders to our appetites. Of course the physical appetites themselves are not evil; indeed, they are God-given and essential for the continuance of human life. God has not given us these things to taunt and trap us. The problem is that our fallen sinful nature so often demands a level of satisfaction which involves breaking God's laws or running to an uncontrolled excess. John is concerned that we should realize that we cannot love the Father and live that way. The body is not evil, any more than the natural world is. That mistake was made by some early Christians, and many others have followed them in it. But what is called *the flesh*, the corrupt nature of men and women, can act as a tyrant over the body and degrade it. The person controlled by these cravings for self-indulgence is not free; he or she is, in fact, the devil's prisoner.

Think, for example, of the alcoholic or the drug addict. That craving that is now out of control started somewhere. It had its beginnings in an extra drink, or an experiment with one or two pills. Those now imprisoned never intended to be wrecked by it, but the craving took them over, until they were no longer in control. In this way, human lives are gradually destroyed. Similarly, those who reject God's instructions regarding his good gift of sex within lifelong marriage imagine that they have set themselves free. They never intend to arrive at a place where meaningful relationships become impossible, where the mechanics of sex take over from any real depth of personal commitment, where love seems to be an empty, mocking illusion. It was all intended to be so natural, liberating and beautiful; but the appetite becomes a tiger, and once God's laws are flouted, it begins to maul us till we are destroyed.

What we need to realize is that the world (and behind it the devil) cannot produce what it offers. Its attractions are fundamentally deceptive. That is why we all need to be warned of the heartbreak and misery that lie on the other side of every act of rebellion against God. It is like drinking salt water. Far from being satisfied, the unquenchable thirst is in fact increased, and that is no way for a child of God to live. So the Christian has to learn to say 'No' to the world's temptations.

Second, John mentions *the lust of the eyes*. Here John directs our attention to the chief bridge between the *flesh* and the outside world. He lived, as we do, in a society where debauchery and violence were often regarded as entertainment. The world is characterized by the desire to see things for the sake of sinful pleasure. In our society with its increased technological capabilities this now reaches alarming proportions, as pornography begins to invade the homes and lives of many children through the widespread use of social media and the Internet. Clearly this is no way for a Christian to live. You cannot love God and the world. But that is only one example. Surely John is also referring to the covetous eyes that say, 'I see it, I want it, I'll have it.' Here is the sin on which the advertising media prey and grow fat. And as Christians living in a wealthy consumer society we need constantly to be judging our own reaction to the covetousness which is characteristic of the world and which so often infects our own attitudes.

Third, John speaks of *the pride of life*. This phrase has at its heart the idea of the illusory glamour of the world, with its concentration on material possessions that decay and empty human glory. Again, we need to be radical in our self-criticism. It is true that God gives us all things richly to enjoy; but they are *his* gifts, and we are to use them as stewards responsible to him for the way we use our master's resources. We dare not boast about them. Yet we Christians are often curiously blind to this form of worldliness. Concern about possessions, status, our image, or perhaps that equally deadly form of pride that apes humility – all these are forms of the pretentiousness of human life apart from God. In such a situation, people are eager to impress, always wanting to be 'one up'. They never let pass a chance in a conversation to make a point that exalts themselves and puts the hearers a little bit lower down the ladder. But that is no way for a Christian to live. It is characteristic of the world, and the world cannot satisfy. Its attractions deceive. This is why we have to be careful of where our daily behaviour is leading us. Too often, when facing temptation, we ask, 'What's wrong with it?' As Christians we really ought to be asking, 'Is there anything right in it?' (see also 1 Cor. 6:12; 10:23).

This leads us to John's other great constraint, which he voices in verse 17a. Not only do the world's attractions fail to satisfy, but they cannot last. All of these desires feed on their own fulfilment, but ultimately none of them will remain. So why should those who are heirs of the eternal world concentrate their interests and ambitions on something that is so fleeting and unreliable? We need to realize the brittleness of this world. Even before death, people who have lived this way are often convinced of the emptiness and uselessness of their lives, and are sometimes profoundly frightened. A millionaire who may have lived for money can take nothing of it beyond the grave. The social climber will never be high enough up the ladder. The good-time girl ends up as a spent alcoholic. The workaholic is made redundant, or forced to retire early. Why live for these things, when they cannot last? We should remember the 'ultimate statistic': one out of one dies.

So John challenges us to make Christian decisions about the way we are living today. If we love the world, we cannot love the Father. If we ally ourselves with this world, we live for what cannot last, and condemn ourselves to be identified with its decay and ultimate judgment. Such choices are part of our human responsibility. John challenges us to ask whose friend we really are: the world's, or God's?

2. A distinct alternative

But whoever does the will of God lives for ever (17b). Clearly, for John, doing the will of God is loving the Father. The antithesis is made very plain. The world attracts and ensnares so many people. They love it and follow its ways, fundamentally because they love themselves and want to indulge themselves. But over against that stands the God who is a loving, heavenly Father, and with him those who show their love for him by their obedience to his will. The world and those who live for it will pass away. The Father and his obedient children will live for ever. All that Satan can offer is desires which will never be satisfied. God has a perfect will that will never be thwarted. The followers of the world share the condemnation and death of its system. The children of God share his eternal life. The challenge that we each face is whether the guiding principle of our life is doing and getting what we want, or obeying God's will and following his purposes. That is the difference between heaven and hell.

But we need also to remember that none of us will get to heaven by trying to do God's will, as though by our own unaided efforts we were able to love God sufficiently to be worthy of being received into his presence. John's Gospel again puts us right on this, when Jesus himself declares, 'The work of God is this: to believe in the one he has sent' (John 6:29). His desire is that no-one should be destroyed, but that all should repent and believe the good news of salvation in Christ. God sent his Son into our world to demonstrate his love for us by overcoming that world through his perfect life of obedience to the Father's will, and by taking our sin and guilt upon himself as he offered up that life to be the atoning sacrifice for our sins. We need not drift on the world's tide towards God's judgment. To do so is to love this world too much. Rightly to understand God's love for this world involves surrendering every part of our own lives to Jesus Christ as Lord. Only such a thoroughgoing commitment can adequately express the love we owe him for all that he has done for us.

1 John 2:18–23

7. Realism about the enemy

John knew that he was involved in a battle for truth, and so are we. If the false teachers gain the upper hand, the Christian church will soon be shorn of her power. If she becomes indistinguishable from the world around her, she and her distorted message will go the way of that world. They will pass away. That is precisely the tragedy we see today in those churches which have progressively deserted the apostolic gospel over the last century and emptied their buildings of worshippers. If this generation of evangelical Christians is not committed to believing, living and passing on God's truth, now while we have the opportunity, there may not be another generation of evangelicals.

But we are tempted to shrug off these warnings because of the relativism of our culture. All around us people are saying, 'It doesn't really matter what you believe so long as you believe it sincerely.' What they mean is that we no longer believe in the truth. We no longer believe in anything objective out there that corresponds to reality (let alone anyone!). All that we know is that we cannot know. So with the enlightenment of contemporary intellectual tolerance, Christians are permitted to believe in God, if they insist, but not to propagate such beliefs or expect others to get involved. It is just one package on the shelves of the ideological supermarket, looking a bit passé these days; but if you like it, you buy it. 'If it's true for you, that's fine; we all have our own beliefs. Sincerity rules, OK?'

Yet who would be content to act on that basis in other areas of life, where the question of right and wrong, truth or falsehood, has more obviously dramatic implications? Suppose you are on a family outing in the countryside. Your little girl spies some juicy, inviting red berries. She sincerely believes they would taste nice, and that such beautiful things could not possibly harm her. Would you encourage your child to act on the basis of the sincerity of her belief?

It is possible to be sincerely wrong. As much as we might like to pretend we live in a world without absolutes, in practice none of us can live that way. Our world and our lives within it are finite. There is a structure of reality that exists, and in the spiritual realm as well as in the physical this means that some beliefs are true and others false. For example, the law of gravity will always apply, however 'sincere' I may be in my delusion that I can deny or ignore it. The apostle's concern here is to instruct us on how we can distinguish the true from the false in practice.

Taking up the theme of verse 17, that the world and its desires are passing away, John speaks in verse 18 of *the last hour.* Did John mean by this that he believed the return of Christ to be imminent? There is no indication of that in the context. *The last hour* matches the New Testament's phrase 'the last days', which refers to the period between the first and second comings of Christ, or more accurately between Pentecost and Christ's return – the final period of time, what others have called the age of the gospel, or of the church. From the divine perspective, there is only one climactic event in history that remains to be accomplished, and that is the return of Christ as King and Judge. The whole period is marked by hostility from the world, sometimes in the form of infiltration of the church with error, sometimes in the form of direct persecution. Towards its end, what we might call the last of the last days, the opposition of these antichristian forces will intensify, in anticipation of the moment of consummation when Christ appears. Until then, Christians are to be on their guard, recognizing the enemy and counteracting his tactics.

1. How to recognize antichrists

Verse 18 speaks of both *the antichrist* and *many antichrists.* John is the only biblical author to use this expression (see also 2:22; 4:3; and 2 John 7), though Jesus himself warned his followers of 'pseudo-Christs': 'For false messiahs and false prophets will appear and perform great signs and wonders to deceive, if possible, even the elect' (Matt. 24:24). Paul also speaks of a 'man of lawlessness' who even proclaims himself to be God (2 Thess. 2:3–4) and in whom the antichristian forces will find their focus before the return of Christ. Interpreters differ as to whether this is a specific individual or an all-pervading ideology. What is clear from the New Testament is that antichristian forces will manifest themselves in their implacable opposition to Christ and his church in every generation.

There are at least two predominant ideas in the use of this term *antichristos*. The first is of a rival to Christ, who claims to possess all the power and ability of Christ. The second is of opposition to Christ, deliberately standing over against Jesus and his righteousness and truth. The antichrist is thus a usurper, who, under false pretences, assumes a position to which he has no right, and who resolutely opposes the rightful owner of that position, Christ. This deception must be detected and opposed in both our belief and our behaviour.

a. Belief (2:22–23)

Who is the liar? It is whoever denies that Jesus is the Christ. Such a person is the antichrist – denying the Father and the Son. The repetition of 'denies' here makes this a very strong statement indeed. Everything depends on what a person believes about Jesus Christ. If an individual does not believe that Jesus of Nazareth was and is the Christ, God's own Son, sent from the Father, then he or she is (literally) against Christ. This means that this person cannot be in a right relationship to God the Father, for he or she is denying the whole basis on which such a fellowship could exist. It is an important test, which must be applied to any religious teaching we may hear.

Historically this has provided the Christian church with her motivation for mission. We do not believe that all roads lead to the light. Those belief systems which deny the deity of Christ are antichrist. This does not mean that no grains of truth can be found in their teaching, or that we should reintroduce the appalling horrors of the Crusaders! But it does mean that millions who are enmeshed in false religions and ideologies are caught up in systems that are lies, and desperately need to hear God's truth.

It means, too, that the church must be on the watch against those who infiltrate its own ranks and yet who deny either the full humanity or the full deity of Christ. The most penetrating and wounding attacks come from within. What the persecution of a Nero could not achieve, the heresy of a Cerinthus can. To deny the second person of the Trinity involves denial of the first. John is making doctrinal statements, separating truth from lies. We are not to allow doctrine to be dismissed as 'cold (or barren) intellectualism' or 'merely cerebral', in favour of emotional experiences.

'False doctrine is a lie; it is the opposite of truth; and no amount of putative devotional experience can substitute for it.'[1] Howard Marshall makes the point incisively when he writes: 'To reduce Jesus to the status of a mere man, or to allow no more than a temporary indwelling of some divine power in him, is to strike at the root of Christianity.'[2]

Verse 23 could hardly be more categorical. You cannot have God without believing in Jesus. Christ himself said, 'I am the way and the truth and the life. No one comes to the Father except through me' (John 14:6). If that route is rejected, there is no other. Simply to believe in one God is not saving faith at all. The God of the Bible is a Trinity. There is only one true God and he is the Father of our Lord Jesus Christ. Without the Son, we cannot know the Father. Those who deny this may use the word 'God', but they cannot know him.

b. Behaviour (2:19)

Ultimately antichrists dissociate themselves from those who hold to orthodox Christian doctrine, but they are extremely dangerous just because they originate from within the church and often take a long time to surface. We may think of the contemporary sects and extremist groups which have done so much damage to the Christian cause. John points out that their eventual apostasy proves that they are not simply confused, untaught Christians. Because they so vigorously oppose the truth, they cannot coexist with strong biblical teaching. Their behaviour confirms the heresy of their beliefs. Of course this does not mean that everyone who leaves a church is antichrist; but when a group separates itself into an elite, holier-than-thou huddle, claiming a deeper understanding or experience than other gospel people, beware. It will not be long before unbalanced teaching begins to lead its adherents away into undisguised error. Once the central truths of the faith are denied, the appetite for Christian fellowship is lost.

2. How to counteract antichrists

Mere recognition of error is not enough. We have to counteract it by firmly holding to and living out the truth – not just giving it intellectual credence,

---

[1] Clark, p. 79.
[2] Marshall, p. 159.

but embracing it and making it the very heartbeat of our lives. It was said of John Bunyan, author of *The Pilgrim's Progress*, that his blood was 'Bibline'; if you cut him, the Bible would flow out of his veins. It is that level of commitment to God's truth by his people that most effectively defeats the antichrist. John's emphatic words in verse 20, *But you* . . ., are the first in a series of counter-attacks which follow in the next few paragraphs (2:27, 'As for you . . .'; 3:2, 'But we know . . .'; 3:5, 'But you know . . .'). The world with its deceptive attractions, and the false teachers with their deceptive doctrines and lifestyle, might easily snare God's children and prevent them from practising God's truth, *but* . . . Verses 19 and 20–21 show us how to resist and overcome in our belief and in our behaviour.

a. Belief (2:20–21)

But you have an anointing. The word is *chrisma*. *Christos* (Christ) is the Anointed One, who has given the *chrisma* to every believer in him. This makes us all *christoi*, anointed ones or Christians. As Paul reminds us in Ephesians 4:7–8, 'To each one of us grace has been given as Christ apportioned it. This is why it says [and here Paul quotes from Ps. 68:18]: "When he ascended on high, he took many captives and gave gifts to his people."' The universal gift of the ascended Christ is the Holy Spirit, whose great ministry is to guide all of God's children into God's truth (John 16:13) through the apostolic testimony. All Christians know the truth because without it they could not be Christian. But the fact that anyone knows it at all is attributable solely to the gift of God's grace, in the person and work of the Holy Spirit. In John's terms, the most inexperienced 'baby' Christian knows enough of the truth to distinguish it from lies. The thrust of verse 21 is therefore to hold on to what you already know, not to give up ground to some new speculative theory or to teaching which actually denies the essentials of the faith. Even when we are assailed by doubts, it is not reasonable to surrender what we do know because there are things we do not know. The answer to doubt lies not so much in faith as in truth. Faith may come to mean a subjective exercise, whereas truth has an objective reality outside of ourselves. We would be fools indeed not to believe it! On that footing we come to doubt our doubts, rather than God's truth.

b. Behaviour (2:19)

We need to make sure that we continue in the fellowship of like-minded Christians. We need one another, not to boost our flagging morale, but to encourage one another on in the things that matter most. If we belong to Christ, then we belong to his people and the mark of belonging is remaining. When the going gets tough, when the grass looks greener on the other side, when our fellow Christians seem not to understand us, when the latest novelty in teaching or experience looks exciting and liberating, then we need God's people. With all our imperfections and idiosyncrasies, we belong to one another because we belong to him. And ultimately we prove the reality of our love by our loyalty.

It is a dangerous hour. There are plenty of hostile forces at work. What we believe does matter, as does our fellowship with other Christians. We need to be realistic about our enemy, but confident in our Saviour. Let the apostle Peter have the last word on the same theme:

> Be alert and of sober mind. Your enemy the devil prowls around like a roaring lion looking for someone to devour. Resist him, standing firm in the faith, because you know that the family of believers throughout the world is undergoing the same kind of sufferings.
> (1 Pet. 5:8–9)

1 John 2:24–29

8. Staying on course as a Christian

Everyone who has ever tried to write a book knows that it is one thing to start, but quite another to finish. There are moments in between when completion (or even continuance!) seems the most unlikely of outcomes. At such times it is important to stay on course, and 'KO KO' is the motto – keep on keeping on. We all find the same experience in living the Christian life. After the thrill of the beginning, when like Bunyan's pilgrim we have felt the aching load of sin and guilt fall from our backs, to be buried, without trace, there often come periods of plodding, when self-discipline is the order of the day, when we need to 'pay the most careful attention . . . to what we have heard, so that we do not drift away' (Heb. 2:1). The picture is a telling one. You have only to tie a careless knot to the bollard, or fail to secure the anchor, for the remorseless force of the tide to bear you away from your moorings on to treacherous rocks.

How am I going to stay on course as a Christian? There is no automatic pilot. Like the hymn-writer, 'I see the sights that dazzle, the tempting sounds I hear.'[1] How am I to make sure that I am not sidetracked by glib talkers or smooth operators, that I really do develop as Christ wants me to, and that his purposes really are accomplished in my life? That is what these verses are all about.

1. Let God's truth remain in you (2:24–25)

Verse 24 in Greek begins with the word *you* in an emphatic position, to contrast with the liars of verses 22–23 who deny that Jesus is the Christ.

---

[1] 'O Jesus I Have Promised', by John E. Bode (1816–74).

The difference has already been made by the grace of God, in bringing us out of darkness into his light through the new birth. We do not have to create it, but to enjoy and preserve it. Six times in these six verses John uses the same verb, usually translated *remain* or 'continue', or in some versions 'abide'. It comes three times here in verse 24. John loves this verb, which means 'to take up a permanent address', or 'to make a settled home'. If we want to keep going and keep growing as Christians then the objective truth of God in Christ and in his written Word has to be allowed to settle in our minds and hearts as its permanent home.

It is not so much that we need to be learning new truth. Novelty in itself can be a great snare. Rather, we need to be learning more deeply and practising more fully the great truths we have been aware of from the start of our Christian experience (*the beginning*). Many of us modern Christians spend comparatively little time allowing the majestic truths of our faith to settle deeply into our consciousness. We spend a lot of time talking about our experience of living the Christian life, but not so much dwelling on the character of God, the person of Christ, his atoning death, his resurrection life, the person and activity of the Holy Spirit, and then our universal human sinfulness, the grace of God in salvation, the process of becoming like Jesus (sanctification) and the hope of glory. These truths exist as living realities, independent of us, but they need to be permanently living in our minds and wills. As with children, we shall need to be fed milk before we can progress to solids, but it is only by feeding on God's truth that we can grow as Christians at all.

'Practice makes perfect,' we say; and it is obvious in many areas of human activity. I see it (and hear it!) as my children practise the piano and trombone. If you want to make a good tennis player you must practise that swing or that serve until it becomes a part of you, so that it is there to call on every time you need it – in the groove. Why don't we think of the Christian life like that? John is telling us that it is only as we make time to let God's Word work deeply in our lives that we shall remain in God. As Leith Samuel has often put it, 'The Spirit of God takes the Word of God to make children of God.'

We can have every confidence in that Word. On a visit to Northern Ireland, I heard of a young man who was serving a long sentence for terrorist offences and who had been taking part in the 'dirty protest'. The only thing left in his cell was a Gideons' Bible and he devoted his time to reading it. But he could not understand its meaning, so he asked to see the prison chaplain, who told him to ask God, the Holy Spirit, to open his spiritual understanding. This he did, and it was not long before he was born again, came off the protest and began to grow rapidly as a Christian. The Word of God had rooted him into Christ, where he remains.

And this is what he promised us – eternal life (25). Although we have learned that the full enjoyment of that life awaits us beyond this world, Isaac Watts was right to sing, 'The men of grace have found glory begun below.'[2] Eternal life begins here and now as the Holy Spirit comes to take up residence within the born-again Christian, planting the life of God within our soul. We can know God, not just know about him. We enter a personal relationship with him through faith which unites us to God now and for ever. The future inheritance is already, in part, a present possession. But the way we remain in God, deepening our knowledge of and love for him, and becoming fruitful Christians, is by ensuring that his truth has the priority in our lives. We shall never outgrow the need for his Word as our daily diet, any more than we outgrow the need for daily food. But for most of us eating is not an end in itself; it is a means to live effectively through the day and get our work done. Its ease of preparation, flavour, appearance or even presentation matters less than that we swallow and digest what we need.

2. Let God's anointing teach you (2:26–27)

Again there is a contrast between the false and the true, the counterfeit and the real. The false teachers wanted to lead Christians astray in order to gain power over them and to conscript them into their own clique. That sort of empire-building still lies behind many of the divisions caused by false teaching today. The Greek word for *lead . . . astray*, from the verb *planaō*, meaning 'to cause to wander', gives us our English word 'planet'. The Greeks contrasted the planets, which they observed to 'wander', with the stars which remained fixed. The flourishing sects and cults of the late twentieth and early twenty-first centuries have often gained impetus by deceiving and deluding uncertain Christians with their extravagant claims and clever theories. The remedy is not just 'Truth' as an absolute, out there. It is also the experience of that Truth inwardly.

---

[2] 'Come, Ye That Love the Lord', by Isaac Watts (1674–1748).

For that, we are dependent on God's *anointing* (27). The *anointing* that a king or priest received in the Old Testament was symbolic of the grace of God being poured out on him to equip him for his task or ministry. John's thought is that New Testament Christians have been equipped with that same grace to live in the truth by the Holy Spirit whom God has poured out on every one of his redeemed people. Just as we were dependent on the Spirit for our initial understanding of the gospel and response to it, so he continues to apply God's truth increasingly in our lives.

> The antidote to falling into false ideas of the Christian faith is to be found in holding fast to the initial statement of Christian truth, given in the apostolic witness, as this is confirmed in our hearts by the anointing given by the Spirit.[3]

It is against this background that we are to understand John's statement *you do not need anyone to teach you* (27). If he meant that they had no need of teaching, he would hardly have written the letter! He has already told them (21) that he is writing to people who know the truth, but they still need to be taught. What he means here is that because the Holy Spirit is the divine teacher given to each and every believer, there is no additional secret 'knowledge' into which they need a gnostic sect leader to initiate them. The Holy Spirit is the author of the apostolic testimony (our New Testament) which is his great teaching tool. If you have God's Word in your hand and God's Spirit in your heart you have everything you need to understand truth and grow in Christ. Don't go on a ceaseless quest for novelty. *Just as it has taught you, remain in him.* The Spirit gives life and freshness to the truth. He revives and restores our spiritual experience as he teaches us what we need to know and enables us to respond in faith that obeys. It is his central task to make Jesus real and precious to us (John 16:14), and so to enable us to remain in him.

3. Let your life be rooted in Christ (2:28–29)

As we see that the secret of Christian perseverance is to remain in Christ, our minds go back at once to the Lord's parable of the vine and the branches in chapter 15 of John's Gospel. There is an organic union between

---

[3] Marshall, p. 164.

the stem and the branch which enables the latter to be fruitful. So it is with the Christian. 'I am the vine; you are the branches. If you remain in me and I in you, you will bear much fruit; apart from me you can do nothing' (John 15:5). This is the only way we can stay on course as Christians and fulfil God's purposes of fruitful living. If this world is passing away (17) and if it is the last hour (18), then we, of all people, should have a clear vision of our future. The Lord Jesus is going to appear; we shall meet him, either with joy or with shame, with anticipation or regret. John's great desire for his dear children is that it may be with 'confidence', a word which implies freedom of speech and joyful access, and not the shame that turns away from him (a better translation than *before him*). There is perhaps a play on words here. God's children should have *parrēsia* (confidence) at his *parousia* (appearing). That can be so only if we continue in him now; but it is the assured outcome of that daily lifestyle. Perhaps our present attitude towards his coming gives us some idea of whether or not we are ready to meet him.

That leads us to verse 29, where John highlights for us the present results of truly remaining in Christ. If I am in Christ, as a branch is in the stem of the vine, then the life of Christ must be flowing through me producing its own characteristic fruit of Christlikeness, or holiness. Being righteous is really being like Jesus. When Paul lists the fruit of the Spirit in Galatians 5:22–23, he is drawing a pen picture of Christ. *He is righteous*; we know that as a fact. The logical consequence of my being in him and his being in me is that my life will be increasingly characterized by doing what is right. The habit of righteousness is the proof of the relationship. This is the ultimate guarantee of reality. *Everyone who does what is right has been born of him.* So the knowing of the fact at the beginning of the verse leads to the recognition of the logical consequence in the second part of the verse. And as if to underline all that he has been saying, John reminds us that the heart of Christian experience is being *born of him*. Of whom? Of the Father, or of Christ? Nowhere else in the Bible are Christians referred to as children of Christ; we are brothers and sisters, but not children (Heb. 2:11). Yet the righteousness which we *know*, referred to in the first part of the verse, must be that which we observed in the earthly life of Jesus. So the pronoun must refer to Christ. But isn't that absolutely characteristic of John's theology? He never thinks of God in relation to human beings without thinking of Christ. And he never thinks of the human nature of Christ without thinking also of his deity. The two are fully and always intertwined, for that is the 'knowledge' which lies at the heart of the faith. For just as the Son always did the Father's will, so the mark of our new life will be that we want to please the Father. The dynamic is all Christ's, but the availability is all ours, provided we draw on his limitless resources, day by day. As we remain in him we can have every confidence that, by God's grace, we shall stay on course right to the end.

1 John 3:1–6

9. Living in God's family

One of the loveliest of God's providences is that we cannot choose our parents. We owe so much to them in every aspect of our make-up, and we might often be tempted to wish that things were other than they are – the nose a little shorter, the temper a little longer, the frame a little lighter. But the fact of the matter is that we cannot avoid being like them. Likeness is the proof of the relationship. It is good at the same time to recognize, even in our genetic inheritance, the overarching sovereignty of God, as King David did. In one of his great psalms of praise he affirms to God, 'You created my inmost being; you knit me together in my mother's womb . . . all the days ordained for me were written in your book before one of them came to be' (Ps. 139:13, 16).

What we all accept in the matter of physical descent, John now applies in terms of our spiritual relationship with our heavenly Father. In this realm equally, likeness is the proof of relationship. If we say we are God's children ('born of him', 2:29) we are to prove it by our godliness. Let us learn from John what that will mean, in practice.

1. A relationship of love with the Father (3:1–2)

John addresses his readers again as 'beloved ones' (*agapētoi*, 2; NIV *Dear friends*), those whom he loves with the same quality of love as God's love for him. It is an especially appropriate term here since we are about to be reintroduced to that divine love and all that it has already accomplished in and for God's people. John is wanting us to grasp how radically different from all other sorts of love God's *agapē* really is. The AV translation,

'Behold, what manner of love the Father hath bestowed upon us', gets nearer than the NIV to the feel of what John wrote here. There is an aorist imperative at the beginning of the verse: 'Look!', 'See!' The force is that we need to take time to contemplate this love and allow its reality to sink down into the depths of our being. It is meant to take our breath away; to startle and amaze us so that we are left gasping, 'What sort of love is this?' The word John uses (*potapos*) originally meant 'of what country?' It is a word that expresses surprise in encountering something foreign, something we are not used to. The disciples use this word in Matthew 8:27, when, amazed by the power of Jesus in stilling the storm on Galilee, they exclaim, 'What kind of man is this? Even the winds and the waves obey him.' He is in a different category from anything we have come across before. And so is the Father's love for us.

It is a love in which he takes all the initiative to make us his children; a love that gives lavishly and freely to those who are utterly undeserving. When we contemplate our sin and rebellion against the background of God's unapproachable light, his total holiness, we begin to sense something of John's wonder that he should ever bother with people like us. Yet the love of God delights to change rebels into children who belong to the family. Not only does he give us his name (*called children of God*, 1), but he gives us his status (*now we are children of God*, 2). This is no wishful thinking, no legal fiction, but an eternal reality.

Rightly to understand this concept of adoption, we have to remember that the choice lay entirely with the Father and was motivated only by his nature of love. Adoption is a legal action by which people take into their family a child who is not their own, who has no rights within that family, in order to give that child all the privileges of their own children. In Roman law, as in ours, an adopted child was entitled to all the rights and privileges of a natural-born child. What might motivate people to do that, potentially at considerable cost to themselves? Perhaps there might be something attractive about the child, or there might be an old friendship with his or her parents, who had died. But the basic motivation would be pity, compassion, love. Love gives. So it is with God, who 'sent his Son, born of a woman, born under the law, to redeem those under the law, that we might receive adoption to sonship' (Gal. 4:4–5). In our case there was nothing attractive or even deserving in us to draw out that love, but God chose to love us, because he is love. This has always been so. Way back in the Old Testament, it was the same principle on which God acted towards

Israel, when he reminded them, 'The LORD did not set his affection on you and choose you because you were more numerous than other peoples . . . But it was because the LORD loved you' (Deut. 7:7–8). All Christians know that it is that sort of love which has reached out towards them through Jesus Christ, lifted them out of sin and brought them into the family of God. Can we express our amazement and gratitude more powerfully than Samuel Crossman did over three centuries ago? He wrote,

My song is love unknown,
　My Saviour's love to me;
Love to the loveless shown,
　That they might lovely be.
O who am I,
　That for my sake
　My Lord should take
Frail flesh, and die?[1]

I suppose it is just because this love is unconditional and limitless that we human beings find it very hard to accept. Many of the Christians I meet have never known a love like that in any other relationship. In childhood they learned that their parents' approval and love had to be earned, by conforming to their dictates and living up to their expectations. And because they could never be good enough, or achieve enough, they were never sure of being accepted. I think of a student friend of mine who rang up his father to tell him of his success in his exams, to be told by his father, 'Good, that means we can still be friends.' Such attitudes cut very deeply into our thoughts and emotions as we are growing up, and it is very easy for us to transfer the same assumption into our relationship with God.

There are many Christians who cannot really accept this lavish love of God for them personally. They are always trying to be good enough to persuade God to love them, rather than accepting the fact that he already does. So they embark on a ceaseless treadmill of Christian activity, always trying to prove to themselves and others that their grades are good enough to pass with God. If we put in sufficient effort, surely he must bless us, we think.

---

[1] 'My Song Is Love Unknown', by Samuel Crossman (c.1624–83).

But actually we pervert the grace of God into a religion of works, and what should be a delight becomes first a duty and then a drudgery. God's grace is not conditioned by whether or not we have scored B+ for our Christian lives this week. He lavishes love on all his children. That does not mean that he spoils us by giving us more than he knows would be good for us, nor that he is undemanding about our service for him or unconcerned about our failings and weaknesses. He loves us too much to let us get away with them! But it is a Father's love, perfect in its understanding and compassion, and exactly suited to the child's personal and individual need.

If he has chosen to make us his children, then he is going to bring us home to heaven. *What we will be has not yet been made known* (manifested). *But we know . . . we shall be like him* (2). That is a process in which he is involved now with every one of his children. He is making us more like the beloved Son, and we must not take things into our own hands as though we can earn that love. It is given. It is pure grace. He establishes the relationship, and to live in this relationship is to grow in the family likeness.

We need to stop our busy Christian lives from time to time, to assess honestly how much of our activity is an expression of love for the Lord who loves us, and how much comes from being driven along by a desire to impress (which reveals a fundamental insecurity), or by group pressures (which dictate whether or not we 'belong'). We need to remind ourselves often that it is our love relationship with the Father that matters most, that what we are is far more significant than what we do. Security comes through realizing that our identity as God's dearly loved children depends not on our activity, but on his electing grace. Our loving Father wants each one of his children to develop to the full his or her unique potential; to be like Jesus.

This confidence will have two practical outworkings, which John mentions in these verses. It will help us to cope both with those details of our faith we cannot yet know and also with the hostility of the world. There are aspects of God's truth which have not yet been revealed, and it is no part of our discipleship to be trying to probe them with our imagination. 'The secret things belong to the LORD our God, but the things revealed belong to us and to our children for ever' (Deut. 29:29). We do not know all the details of what heaven will be like, and we do not need to know. We do not know how the resurrection body will be raised, or what it will be like. All that will be revealed when Christ is revealed, *when* he *appears* (2). What we do know is that he is coming, that we are going to see him as he truly is; and in that moment, by the same grace that has made us his children, we shall be made like him. At that moment the process which began when first we trusted Christ will come to its fulfilment, and the image of God in his children will be fully restored.

Such assurance is a very important ingredient in our living for Christ in a hostile world, for its persecution should only turn out to increase our certainty. *The reason the world does not know us is that it did not know him* (1). Of course in one sense the world does know us. It knows we are here, just as it knew Christ during his earthly ministry. What it does not know is that Christians are God's children. It has no idea of the love relationship that exists in daily fellowship between the Lord and his people. Such a concept is dismissed as a delusion. We should not expect the world to want to know.

If we look at the pattern of Christ's ministry we can see that there were times when he seemed overwhelmingly popular, when multitudes hung on his words, but in reality they were following him for what they could get out of it, and all but a handful had deserted him by the end. Though the crowds seemed at one point to know him, 'Jesus would not entrust himself to them, for he knew all people' (John 2:24). During his Jerusalem ministry he challenged the temple crowds, 'Yes, you know me, and you know where I am from. I am not here on my own authority, but he who sent me is true. You do not know him' (John 7:28). The world of unbelieving people can have only false ideas and concepts regarding the heavenly Father and his dear children. Let us not be surprised if the media pass over the biblical gospel as old-fashioned, unoriginal, boring. Of course we are to seize all the opportunities we can to make Christ known by every means available, but we should not expect it to be peak-time viewing, or the front-page story. *The world does not know.*

What we must remember is that this world has an end point. History is working towards a climax, when Jesus will appear. This future fact is both a great hope and a great stimulus. The Prince of Wales, as heir to the throne, lives already in the light of what he will be one day. He does not yet possess his full inheritance, but his whole life has been, and is, shaped by it. One day we shall be like Jesus, changed into his likeness. Meanwhile, we live today in the enjoyment of the privileges of grace as his adopted children, knowing that on that day we need have nothing to fear ('confident') and nothing to hide ('unashamed', 2:28). Knowing our future does give confidence. But it does not make Christians complacent. It makes us concerned to do all we can now, in his strength, to live up to what we are and to what we shall be. That leads us to John's next thought.

2. A responsibility of trust from the Father (3:3)

John returns to a theme which he outlined in 2:29: the new relationship brought about by God's love through the new birth will show itself in the practical evidence of a righteous life. So here, the conviction that we are God's children leads to a practical programme developing personal holiness. If all our future expectation is centred on Christ, then we shall want to be as much like him as we can be now. If heaven is the destination, we must be travelling the road that leads there. Notice how carefully John rules out any exceptions. This applies to every Christian (*all*). The present tense, *purify*, is significantly chosen too, indicating a continuous process which is to be taking place at this moment. 'He who stops purifying himself has dropped this hope from his heart.'[2] That present tense also guards against any incipient perfectionism, which might want to claim that we can reach a stage in this world when we no longer need to grow in holiness.

In linking holiness to our hope, John is seeking to stimulate our motivation to live differently. 'Hope springs eternal in the human breast,' according to Alexander Pope, and certainly human life is driven and moulded largely by hope for the future. Material ambitions of wealth and status may drive us to devote our talents, time and energy to achieving success. Think of the dedication of a world-class athlete, the degree of sacrifice, the output of resources, to achieve fleeting fame and perhaps fortune (see 1 Cor. 9:24–27). These goals are not only difficult to attain, they are impossible to keep. Yet the Christian's hope, by contrast, is secure and unfading, 'an inheritance that can never perish, spoil or fade . . . kept in heaven for you' (1 Pet. 1:4). Ought not our motivation to be correspondingly great? For we do have a responsibility to purify ourselves. This is the other side of the coin of God's rich love and free mercy which we have been considering. To claim the hope of heavenly glory and yet be unconcerned about sin in our own lives, by disobedience or not practising the truth, is in fact to be walking in darkness.

---

[2] Lenski, p. 453.

How then are we to fulfil the responsibility? John points us to the Lord Jesus. Not that he purified himself, for he *is* pure. It is his inherent quality. But he demonstrated that purity in the same hostile world in which his children are called to develop theirs. He set himself always to do the Father's will even though he knew that it would frequently and ultimately be a path of suffering. God's law was written on his heart, and to that law the human Jesus was always loyal and true. Because of that law, his life was devoted to love for his Father and for his world. This was why he took the form of a servant and humbled himself to death on the cross. If *he* 'learned obedience from what he suffered' (Heb. 5:8), should we not give ourselves to a similar daily, disciplined obedience? Only God the Holy Spirit can make us holy, and this is God's will (1 Thess. 4:3). But our cooperation is essential, and that is seen in the dedication of our lives to our Lord and our readiness to respond to him in loving obedience at every turn of the way.

3. A reflection of the Father in our lifestyle (3:4–6)

Again John returns us to his insistence that living as children of God means a clean break with sin. These verses are very straightforward indeed. Every time we sin we break God's law, which is a reflection of his perfect character and will. Any deviation from God's instructions is an act of lawlessness, which shows our heart attitude towards God. It flaws our life, just as one stone thrown up from the road can shatter a car's windscreen and bring a driver to a rapid halt. Think for a moment of the parallel with human law, which may, or may not, reflect the law of God. Sometimes a person will quite consciously and deliberately flout that law, as in a case of theft or fraud. On other occasions the law may be broken accidentally, as when a stranger finds himself driving the wrong way down a one-way street. Yet in either case an offence is committed; sin is lawlessness. The false teachers seem to have been claiming that they lived on a super-spiritual plane, well above any sort of law or rules, and so the Christian was free to 'know' God, without keeping the commandments. John goes behind the idea that sin is the contravention of this or that specific law, to show that it is an attitude towards God, of which every sinner is guilty.

The first coming of Jesus is seen by John to be God's remedy for the problem of human sin (5), by taking our sins away. John, the apostle, learned that first from John the Baptist, who proclaimed Christ as God's Lamb (John 1:29). Jesus taught the same truth by proclaiming himself as the Good Shepherd who would lay down his life for the sheep (John 10:15). Only in its death could the lamb become a sacrifice for sin, though it had to be spotless in order to be acceptable to God. In the same way, John reminds us of the sinless perfection of Christ, but sees that as a necessary element in his atoning death. Only someone who was sinless in himself could atone for the sins of others. And here was the difference between Christ, God's Lamb, and all the other sacrifices brought throughout the centuries of Israel's history. Their bodies had to be without blemish as they became the substitute for the sinner, but none of those animal sacrifices could ever bring moral perfection to the altar, by definition. The glory of Christ is that he was able to bring a sinless human *will* and to offer that in the place of our rebellious sinful wills, as his blood flowed for our sins at Calvary. That is why the cross is the heart of the Christian message. It is God's answer to our deepest need. God longs to bring human beings back into his family, but sin is inconsistent with sonship. So God comes in the person of Jesus, the Son, to uphold his own moral law, throughout his life and eventually at the expense of his own life, in order to take away our sins and make forgiveness a reality.

The important question, in the light of the cross, then becomes, 'Have my sins been taken away?' Verse 6 tells us that the answer lies in our present experience. Do I keep on sinning, or is my life distinctively different? 'Look at your lifestyle,' is John's message. There may be key moments of change to look back to, in a response at an evangelistic meeting, the signing of a commitment card, or events such as baptism or being received as a member of a local church, which all have their place in our spiritual pilgrimages. Nevertheless John does not ask us about those; he simply says, 'Do you keep on sinning?' The person who does has not yet seen or known Christ, in that personal way that is described in verse 6 as 'living in him'. If Jesus was sinless and came to this world expressly to take away our sins, how can sin be cherished by anyone who is really living in Christ?

It is important to remember that John is not for one moment saying that a true Christian never sins. He has already warned us against that error (1:8, 10) and reminded us of the means God has provided for our cleansing and restoration (1:9; 2:1). Although Christians fail and fall, they can be forgiven. But we are to remember that such forgiveness is at the expense of the lifeblood of the Son of God. Grace is free, but it is not cheap. The mark of true gratitude is that we do not keep on sinning.

F. F. Bruce has a helpful illustration at this point.

When a boy goes to a new school, he may inadvertently do something out of keeping with the school's tradition or good name, to be told immediately, 'That isn't done here.' A literalist might reply, 'But obviously it *is* done; this boy has just done it' – but he would be deliberately missing the point of the rebuke. The point of the rebuke is that such conduct is disapproved of in this school, so anyone who practises it can normally be assumed not to belong to the school. There may be odd exceptions, but that is the general rule, which has been verified by experience.[3]

The implications for us are clear. Fellowship with a sinless Saviour and continuance in our sins (keeping on sinning) are mutually contradictory. No compromise is possible. And the logical conclusion we are to draw is that we cannot expect to be confident on that day when we see Christ if we are complacent about sin in our lives here and now.

---

[3] Bruce, p. 90.

1 John 3:7–10

10. Be what you are

I was talking to a casual acquaintance about the Christian faith, and in the course of conversation we discovered that we had a common friend. 'Now he is what I call a *real* Christian,' was the response. I was intrigued and pressed a little further as to what he meant. 'He's always ready to help, to do a good turn for anyone,' the reply came, 'and he isn't dogmatic about what he believes. He doesn't expect you to believe it too!'

But is that a real Christian? Millions of people would offer similar definitions, no doubt; but it is vitally important that people find out God's definition, since on this our eternal future hangs. This is John's overriding concern in this part of his letter. The false teachers who had infiltrated and divided the churches laid great claim to be true Christians, but were they? Doubtless there was a good deal of ferment and discussion among the churches regarding their true position, since they had seemed to be so much a part of the Christian fellowships (2:19).

From 2:29 through to 3:10 John is drawing a series of pictures of two contrasting groups of people, a series which comes to its climax in verse 10. There are those who do right (2:29) and those who keep on sinning (3:4–5). There are those who live in Christ and those who have neither seen nor known him (3:6). There are those who do what is right (3:7) and those who do what is sinful (3:8). There are those who do not continue to sin (3:9) and those who do not do right and do not love their brothers and sisters (3:10). By 3:8 the two groups can be more closely defined and identified as two families of people, with two heads: the children of God and the children of the devil. These very practical facts, which must be applied if we are to know we are truly of God, all centre on the way we live. In establishing this criterion, John is following not simply the logic of common sense and experience, but also the teaching of his Master: 'Watch out for false prophets . . . By their fruit you will recognise them' (Matt. 7:15–16).

1. A principle that distinguishes (3:7–8a)

Little children are easily led astray. Their trusting nature and comparative inexperience of life make them vulnerable targets for those who want to exploit them. John can see this danger among the new generation of Christians in the churches he knows. The problem is that we tend to use the wrong standards by which to assess false teaching. We look at the personalities of teachers rather than their characters. They seem such nice people, so pleasant and affable, so caring and concerned, so ready to share their exciting new visions or ideas. 'They come to you in sheep's clothing, but inwardly they are ferocious wolves,' Jesus warns us (Matt. 7:15). Without doubt the gnostic teachers had great appeal. Their system of truth was an intriguing intellectual construction that seemed to build beyond the rather simple approach of the apostolic message. They were doubtless accomplished orators and attractive personalities, or they would not have had such rapid success. But by adding to God's truth their own imaginative fictions they were destroying the gospel. The extra knowledge they claimed was not a divine revelation, because it did not produce a life of righteousness.

Within certain spiritual people, it was claimed, there was a divine potential or 'spark' which could be ignited by the secret knowledge when they received it. With this knowledge the pure spirit would be able to escape from the prison-house of the body at death, and, dodging all the hostile demons, wing its way to be reunited with God. Salvation therefore depended on knowledge, not on grace. It was open, then, to a certain elite, but not to anyone who might desire it. One can see immediately its appeal to intellectual pride and social snobbery. To be on the inside, one of the 'illuminated', would be a great attraction. It still is today. To be a few rungs up the ladder still has a powerful appeal to our fallen sinful humanity. This is part of the appeal of the Christian sects and sub-Christian cults that have multiplied in recent decades all over the world. But does it lead to godliness? That is John's principle.

For some followers of Gnosticism it led to gross immorality. Insisting that their special knowledge made them 'pearls' which could not be sullied by any 'mud' of this world, and that to the 'spiritual' person no action is defiling, they gave themselves up to self-indulgence. Others followed a more ascetic line of thought and were consumed by their own pride and imagined superiority. But John insists on the principle that actions are an infallible guide to character. Jesus 'went around doing good . . . because God was with him' (Acts 10:38). What was true of the Lord Jesus, that he demonstrated his righteous nature in a life of righteous behaviour, is to be true of his genuine disciples too. It is not that we are accepted by God because we do what is right, for 'all our righteous acts are like filthy rags' (Isa. 64:6), but because Christ's righteousness has been put to our account, through his atoning death, and we are justified by faith. To this we must add, however, that the marks of being justified will be seen in our behaviour. If we truly belong to Christ, we shall show his righteous character.

That means testing our lives and those who claim to teach God's truth by the infallible Word which God has already spoken in Scripture. Anyone can make extravagant claims to have received special knowledge through an experience of divine enlightenment, just as anyone can claim to have become a Christian. The test is in such people's lives. To which family do they show themselves to belong? Jesus told some very religious Jewish leaders that their father was not Abraham, or God, as they claimed, but the devil (John 8:44). His reasoning was that, in spite of all their fine words and outward devotion to God, their actions proclaimed it:

> If you were Abraham's children . . . then you would do what Abraham did. As it is, you are looking for a way to kill me, a man who has told you the truth that I heard from God . . . If God were your Father, you would love me, for I have come here from God. I have not come on my own; God sent me.
> (John 8:39–40, 42)

Their murderous behaviour, stemming from their unwillingness to receive God's truth, was inescapable proof of their family allegiance. They were the devil's children; like father, like son. So John warns his dear children not to be led astray by mere words, but to look beyond them to the actions which reveal the speakers' true identities.

2. A power that destroys (3:8b–10)

John defines the purpose of the incarnation as destructive. Christ came to 'loose' (NIV *destroy*) the works of the devil. The verb (*lyō*) means, at root, to untie and so to set free, and is used of the colt on which Jesus made his kingly entry into Jerusalem (Matt. 21:2) or of Lazarus's grave clothes being unwound when Jesus raised him up (John 11:44). But it also came to be used of breaking something up into its component parts, tearing down a building, for example, and so destroying it. This gives us John's meaning here in terms of doing away with the devil's works, demolishing them and bringing them to an end. This was why Jesus came.

In passing, we should note that this gives us an important key in dealing with the frequently posed problem of the origin and purpose of evil. Taking verse 8, *the devil has been sinning from the beginning*, as an example, people often ask, 'Why?' Did God not foresee that this would happen? And if he did, why does he allow it? Is he not powerful enough to stop it? Or does he not care? We have only a short space here to deal with a fundamental and wide-ranging human dilemma, but John does give us some real help. He affirms, in common with the rest of the Bible,[1] that the devil is a created being, a highly superior spiritual intelligence, who chose to rebel against God's authority, to seek to usurp his throne and to set himself up as a rival ruler of the universe. In his rebellion evil finds its origin. The devil was the first sinner, and sinners today, without Christ, are his posterity.

Though we cannot probe the mysteries of God's purposes, we cannot believe for one moment that this chain of events took him by surprise, or produced an emergency in heaven. Otherwise, what would we make of Peter's assertion that Christ, the lamb, was 'chosen before the creation of the world' (1 Pet. 1:20), or Paul's affirmation that Christians are chosen in Christ 'before the creation of the world' (Eph. 1:4)? Having created the angels and later human beings to worship and love him (both of which are free responses), God knew that his creatures would choose wrongly and, starting on a disastrous course of rebellion, open the pathway to perdition. He could have destroyed evil in a moment, but where would that have left us? Bringing it right up to date, where would we want God to begin and end? Imagine two cars on a collision course, one being driven by a

---

[1] See, for example, Job 1 – 2; Isa. 14:12–15; Heb. 2:14–15; Rev. 20:7–10.

drunkard. Do we expect God to immobilize the car, to cause it to change course miraculously? Or do we want to live in a world where causes lead to effects, where people are responsible for their actions? Would we want God to 'deal with' evil by striking us dumb if we began to tell a lie?

We begin to see a different aspect of God's grace when we think in these terms. In that grace, God came in the person of the Lord Jesus to shoulder the moral guilt of a world that has gone awry and is on a course of self-destruction. On the cross he suffered, bled and died, in place of sinners like us, so that we might be forgiven, reborn, transformed. God had a greater purpose on hand than snuffing evil out, and with it all that he had created; he meets it face to face, conquers it in Christ's death and resurrection, and transcends it by his grace and love.

So the coming of Christ, culminating in his cross, spells God's total triumph over all the hostile forces which have tied us in knots and bound us in chains of sin which we cannot loose. Christ not only sets the captives free, but destroys the captor. He shared our humanity 'so that by his death he might break the power of him who holds the power of death – that is, the devil – and free those who all their lives were held in slavery by their fear of death' (Heb. 2:14–15). No wonder this risen, ascended Lord Jesus proclaimed to John, in his Patmos vision of glory, 'I hold the keys of death and Hades' (Rev. 1:18b).

Why then do we see the devil still at work today? Here again the rest of the New Testament helps us. The victory has been won, but its full implementation awaits the completion of God's purposes in bringing every son and daughter home to glory, and of building his church in every place. Until that time, God extends his grace and mercy to all, and today remains a 'day of salvation' (2 Cor. 6:2). As Paul teaches us,

Then the end will come, when he [Christ] hands over the kingdom to God the Father after he has destroyed all dominion, authority and power. For he must reign until he has put all his enemies under his feet. The last enemy to be destroyed is death . . . When he has done this, then the Son himself will be made subject to him who put everything under him, so that God may be all in all.
(1 Cor. 15:24–26, 28)

But let's get back to the nitty-gritty of everyday Christian experience in this world. What are we to do about the devil's continuing activity in our own lives, through the temptations of the world and the flesh? If the test of real spirituality is the way we behave, Christ must enable us to live differently. And this is the force of verse 9. Christ came to destroy the devil's work in us, so that we might live lives that are distinctively different, lives that are not given to sin, but which become increasingly like Jesus. That potential is in Christ and is available to everyone who has been *born of God*. As a father's *seed* is within his child, so, when a person is born again, the life of God is implanted within that life. 'God's nature abides in him' (rsv), and this is the power by which Satan's work in our lives will be undone and ultimately abolished. The new birth involves such a radical change at the heart of our experience that, whereas sin used to come naturally to us, now it is unnatural to continue to sin.

Again, we need to understand very carefully just what John is meaning when he states in verse 9b that the Christian *cannot go on sinning*. We must not forget what John has already taught us about the fact that no Christian is sinless. We must balance that truth with the equivalent understanding that no Christian is a habitual sinner either. While we are not to expect perfection, on the one hand, neither are we to settle for a mediocre level of Christian experience, on the other.

Here is a man (shall we say) with a foul temper who becomes a Christian. That man finds that he can no longer go on losing his temper without concern. He does lose it from time to time, but he is always convicted of his sin and led through confession to Christ's cleansing and forgiveness. Gradually he begins to gain the victory over his temper. The life of God within him begins to expel and destroy the old habits and characteristics. He is being changed. The speed and depth of the change will largely depend on the extent to which he allows the Holy Spirit to control each area of his life. What is true for something outwardly visible, like a fiery temper, is equally true for those more common but hidden sins of criticism, jealousy, bitterness, greed and impurity, which dog so many of our lives. If we are unconcerned about them, excusing them as our little weaknesses or peccadilloes, we can only be grieving (Eph. 4:30) and quenching the Spirit (1 Thess. 5:19). We are denying our new birth. No real Christian can rest content with that state of affairs. We cannot be happy to go on sinning.

Indeed, we need not! For the warning of verse 9 is also a great encouragement. The Spirit wars against the flesh in every believer's life, but we are not involved in an unequal struggle with evil. The Lord is going to win. We are in living contact with the Conqueror, and all his resources are always available. If it is true that only Christ can live a righteous life, it is also true that his life is implanted in us, when we are born again. When we sin it is because we are failing to allow Christ's risen life in all its power to flow into our thoughts and motives, our circumstances and experience, bringing us his victorious resurrection power. A house with an electricity supply has constant access to a powerful energy source. What we must do to enjoy the benefit of that is plug in and switch on!

Verse 10 both summarizes what has gone before and, in its final clause, leads on to John's next topic. The righteousness that demonstrates our membership of God's family is not cold and clinical. It is inseparable from love. The God who is light is also love. Love is righteousness in relationship with others – not primarily an emotion, but an act of will. It is not feeling warm towards other people in a general way, but doing good to specific individuals. Love as a feeling only is useless. No marriage can survive on feelings. Love has to be expressed in caring and sharing, in hard work and loyalty, in generosity and long-suffering. That's the love without which we have no right to claim to be God's children. Of course it is superhuman. It does not grow naturally in this world's soil. It is the gift of God. But where it exists, there is positive proof of the life of God in the souls of men and women, and so of authentic membership of God's family.

1 John 3:11–18

11. A faith that is real

John is continuing his exposition of how Christians may know that eternal life is theirs. As we climb the spiral staircase of John's thought, we gain different perspectives on the assurance and confidence that he repeatedly stresses. Earlier he wrote about 'truth' ('God is light') – we can know that what we believe is true. Now his emphasis is on 'love' – our love for our fellow Christians confirms that our faith is real. Verse 14 sums up this paragraph with its assertion that love for one another is an indispensable mark of genuine Christianity.

Faith and love belong together throughout the New Testament. For Paul they are the essential evidence of genuineness, in which he frequently rejoices as he contemplates the churches to which he writes.[1] So much so that in Galatians 5:6 he states, 'The only thing that counts is faith expressing itself through love.' For his part, John's concern is to explore and develop what love for one another means in practice. He does this by continuing to draw contrasting pictures. We noted in verse 10 the two family groupings of humanity – children of the devil or children of God – and John now expounds the basic attitudes and actions of each. The former family is represented by Cain, and the latter by Christ.

1. Two basic attitudes

If you are carrying a cup which is filled to the brim and someone jogs your arm, whatever is in the cup spills out. The unexpected knocks and

---

[1] See, for example, Eph. 1:15; Col. 1:4; 1 Thess. 1:3; 1 Tim. 1:3–5.

irritations of life are similarly a very good indicator of the quality of the life within. How do we habitually react towards other people? Are we like the message I read on a student's sweatshirt: 'I love mankind; it's people I can't stand'? More importantly: as a Christian, how do I react to my brothers and sisters in God's family? *We should love one another*, says John (11), establishing that this is foundational to all genuine Christianity. Just as it is not simply God's habit to love but the very essence of his being, so 'a person cannot come into a real relationship with a loving God without being transformed into a loving person'.[2] If Christ loved even his enemies (Rom. 5:8–10), can we not love our brothers and sisters in Christ, who have the same heavenly Father and who share the same divine life?

By contrast, John turns to a representative figure from the other family – *Cain*, whose story is recorded in Genesis 4. Instead of loving *his brother*, Abel, Cain's attitude was dominated by a hatred which eventually drove him to kill his brother. At the heart of this hatred lay not simply a personal dislike of Abel, but a moral battle, which Cain lost (12b). Surely we are to suppose that their parents would have told both boys about the Garden of Eden as they grew up. They would have known about the reality of the fall, the eviction from Paradise, and the flaming sword that guarded the way to the tree of life. We can deduce from Abel's actions in Genesis 4:4 that they had at least been instructed that God could be approached only by the way of sacrifice, and that this was his gracious provision by which they could draw near. This principle may well be implicit already in Genesis 3:21. But Cain decided to offer God 'some of the fruits of the soil' (Gen. 4:3). It was an offering that did not really cost him anything, that did not take into account the seriousness of sin, and that was not offered in a spirit of submission and penitence. In that sense his actions were evil, and God was displeased. Even when God explained his response and pleaded with Cain ('If you do what is right, will you not be accepted?', Gen. 4:7), he stubbornly refused to accede to God's demands. He was in a state of rebellion against God and refused to recognize his authority. His anger stemmed from the fact that his own offering was rejected, and his hatred was directed to Abel, as the nearest representative of obedience to God. When God tried to reason with him that this was not a matter of favouritism but of simple right and wrong, obedience and rebellion, all this was spurned. There was a conflict of wills. Cain's life became the battleground.

---

[2] Marshall, p. 212.

'If you do not do what is right, sin is crouching at your door; it desires to have you, but you must rule over it' (Gen. 4:7b). But Cain did not rule over it. His anger against God boiled over against his brother and he killed Abel. *And why did he murder him? Because his own actions were evil and his brother's were righteous* (12b).

That conflict still rages in every human life. Is it to be God's will or mine? Am I going to obey him or run my life as I want to? When I was a schoolteacher one teenager captured this spirit graphically in the opening sentence of an English essay. 'I may make a mess of my life,' he wrote, 'but at least it will be my own mess.' The Gnostics were wrong when they identified our greatest problem as ignorance; it is rebellion.[3] This explains why Christians should *not be surprised* when their love is met with hatred (13). The cosmic conflict still continues. Hatred is still the world's currency. All round the world Christian brothers and sisters are being persecuted, imprisoned, even martyred at this very time by followers of ideologies that are implacably opposed to God and his commandments. We should not be surprised. 'It is the way the Master went; / should not the servant tread it still?'[4]

2. Two representative actions

Verse 12 traces the murder of Abel to Cain's hatred, and verse 15a teaches us that the action is the outcome of the attitude. The Lord Jesus took his penetrating judgment to that level of inner attitude when he warned that 'anyone who is angry with a brother or sister will be subject to judgment' (Matt. 5:22). Human law can judge only actions we have committed, but God judges our motives. The hater and the killer share a common motive. There is no difference in their moral character. Therefore anyone who holds on to a spirit of bitter hatred and hostility towards a brother or sister cannot possibly be at the same time indwelt by the life of the Holy Spirit of God. The life of the Eternal is evidently not there. Of course, murderers may repent and find God's free forgiveness; their sin is not unforgivable. But people cannot claim to have genuine saving faith if they destroy a brother or sister, whether it is that person's physical life or reputation and character.

---

[3] See Paul's diagnosis in Rom. 1:18–22.
[4] 'Go, Labour On; Spend and Be Spent', by Horatius Bonar (1808–89).

Verse 16, by contrast, depicts the representative action of a child of God, seen in the person of the beloved Son. If hatred ultimately reveals itself in murder, love, taken to its conclusion, reveals itself in sacrifice. Love does not destroy another's life, whether in thought or deed. Love gives its own life so that another may live. *Jesus Christ laid down his life for us* demonstrates God's definition of love. It is not mere sentiment or emotion, not simply words, but deeds. And the deeds are not empty gestures; they actively transform the situation. Jesus laid down his life as a ransom price, so that we might be set free.

And when we have been liberated, what then? *We ought to lay down our lives for our brothers and sisters* (16b). This does not mean that a Christian can die for his or her brother or sister in the sense that Jesus did, in order to purchase forgiveness. His death was unique, and was totally sufficient for every sinner's forgiveness and every captive's release. But if love like that really wins our hearts and brings us to repent and to trust our lives to Christ, we shall want to express that same quality of love in our devotion to our fellow Christians. It is a love that gives without counting the cost, without any thought of return, without first weighing up whether or not such love is deserved – a love that is entirely without self-interest. It is the nature of God's love to give, just as it is the nature of the sun to shine. And *that* love is the mark of a faith that is real. It touches our bank accounts and our diaries. It governs the stewardship of our time and talents, our energy and our possessions. Love 'always protects, always trusts, always hopes, always perseveres. Love never fails' (1 Cor. 13:7–8a).

What we need to grasp is that love like this is always available from Christ, who is its only source. We do not have to look into our poverty-stricken selves to generate a love like that. The more we are open to receive it, the more Christ's love will flood into our lives and overflow to others. As Zig Ziglar said, 'Your attitude . . . will determine your altitude.' I think the apostle John would agree!

John soon brings us down to earth, however, with another practical application of these lofty principles in verse 17. We may never be called upon to risk our lives for another Christian, but what about the comparatively minor opportunities we do have for showing love? If we ignore them, how can we believe that our love for God is genuine? After all, this is where it really counts. Every time we come across a genuine case of a Christian in need, our love for God is tested. If we have more than he or she has we shall want to share what we have with our less fortunate friend.

It may be a gift of money, but it may equally be a gift of time, or work on his or her behalf. I know Christians who, in case of family illness, provide meals day after day, or care for children in their homes so that they do not have to be separated from incapacitated parents. Such practical care and help is worth much more than words about love. So John exhorts himself and us (18) not to be loving with the empty evidence of words, but with the genuine evidence of actions. Stretched as I am in a busy pastorate, I am only too conscious of how easy it is to love in words – to express sympathy, to promise to pray, to exhort and encourage – but it is actions that confirm or deny their truth. Without these, our words can be mere hypocrisy. In that case, they do stem not so much from love as from habit or duty. 'It is love "in deed and truth" that is expected from a child of God, not the kind of pious talk that devalues the currency of heavenly love because it is unmatched by corresponding action.'[5]

3. Two contrasting destinies

They are summed up in verse 14. Every Christian has a new destiny: *we have passed from death to life*. This is the content of what we know. The reason *we know* it is that *we love each other*. This life is eternal not only in that it is everlasting, but in that it is the life of God (the Eternal) within us. The alternative is not just physical death – that is merely the symptom. The real death is the awfulness of eternal separation from God, who is the only source of life, light and love; that living death which the Bible calls hell. The reality of my gratitude for my deliverance from this death is evidenced by how much I love my brothers and sisters. God wants to produce the fruit of the Spirit (Gal. 5:22–23) in the life of every member of his family.

---

5 Bruce, p. 97.

1 John 3:19–24

12. How to please God

We live in a generation and a society where nothing goes unquestioned. The surest convictions of the past are bound to be challenged tomorrow, if not today. Sometimes one is tempted to feel that such speculation is the product of academic inbreeding, where research degrees are built and reputations made by theories about theories about theories, at two or three removes from reality. Nevertheless, questions are here to stay, so we can be fairly certain of continuing uncertainty in many areas of life. Christians are not immune from such pressures, especially in an age like our own. Most of us find that we have problems with assurance at some stage of our spiritual pilgrimage. Indeed, having studied John's demanding and penetrating teaching up to this point, it would not be surprising if we faced exactly that problem now. It is appropriate, therefore, that the sensitive, experienced apostle of the love of God should break off for a moment here to deal with two challenges, or even threats, to our assurance that we do belong to God's family and do have eternal life. They still generate much heart-searching, use up a good deal of spiritual and nervous energy, and occupy a fair amount of pastoral counselling time in contemporary church life.

1. The challenge of a condemning heart (3:19–22a)

As I have studied this letter in depth over the past few years I have sometimes found myself beginning to wonder whether I have made any progress at all in the Christian life. The letter is written to give us assurance, but not infrequently it brings us to see how little like our Lord we really are and how much further we have to go. As Christians, we find that *our hearts* do often *condemn us*. Like a judge who discerns something in the prisoner which he or she must expose and sentence, our hearts judge us. We alone know our own inner motives and how often our love for our brothers and sisters, perhaps especially for a particular brother or sister, falls far short of what it ought to be. Our hearts know things about ourselves that are unknown to others, and their condemnation, unlike the accusations of Satan, is not false.

John does not encourage us to deny these things, or to shrug them off, but urges us to meet their challenge by seeing that God knows more. *God is greater than our hearts, and he knows everything* (20b). It is not that God minimizes or disregards our failures. In fact he knows them better than we do, for he sees and understands us even more deeply than we can ever know ourselves. He knows exactly where we are spiritually: our strengths and weaknesses, our gains and losses, our successes and failures. Our comfort is that God knows that the measure of love we do have is irrefutable evidence of the activity of the Holy Spirit in our lives, that we have been born of God, that we have crossed over from death to life. And he wants us to know it too.

Yes, we are imperfect. Our own hearts cry out for a more consistent Christlike love, but that does not destroy our assurance; it confirms it. Some sensitive souls desperately fear that they may have blasphemed against the Holy Spirit and so be beyond the reach of God's forgiveness. A counsellor can bring them relief by helping them to see that their very concern is evidence that they are not guilty of that sin (see Matt. 12:31). In the same way we can counsel our own hearts that our sad dissatisfactions are actually the product of spiritual life. Like John Wesley we often find ourselves praying, 'Lord, cure me of my intermittent piety and make me thoroughly Christian.' This has been the common experience of many believers down the centuries. So, when we face the crisis of a condemning conscience, our hearts are set at rest in the assurance that we can trust ourselves to the mercy of the God who knows us better than we know ourselves, the one who *knows everything*.

This seems to me the most helpful way of tackling the admittedly difficult question of what *This* refers to in verse 19a. It may refer back to the performance of the command to love in deed and truth (in verse 18) but it seems more likely that it begins a new thought. Certainly this interpretation accords with John's frequent insistence that our assurance is based not on our subjective feelings, but on God's truth and love at work within us.

The end result of such assurance is *confidence* (21), which is essential if we are to come *before God* in prayer. I do not think John is saying in verse 21, 'Some Christians never have a condemning heart, so they can be confident before God.' Rather, his meaning is that when we deal with our condemning heart on the grounds of God's truth and love – even though it recurs a dozen times a day – we can become sure that the Lord accepts us in spite of all our faults, and that we can therefore come to him in prayer. We do not need to fear. We can come boldly and meet God face to face. We can pour out our hearts to him and be absolutely frank and honest, completely open about our needs and requests.

Such confidence is vital if we are to pray effectively. It is easy for us to become so tight and tense about our failures, to be so hard on ourselves for not being better, and so miserable about our state, that we lose the sunshine of God's love. Often this is a form of inverted pride. But if we are really resting in Christ, we shall ask great things from God and receive them (22a). Our assurance then is built not only on the promises of God's Word, wonderful and gracious as they are, but on the fact that God treats us as his dearly loved children, day after day, by answering our prayers. We need to learn to revel in that relationship.

But the second part of verse 22 presents us with another area of doubt or challenge.

2. The challenge of an imperfect obedience (3:22b–24)

If our receiving answers to prayer is dependent on our obedience and doing what pleases God (*because*, 22), how can we ever have confidence to pray? Our obedience is always imperfect, and there are many remnants of the old way of life, even in the most holy Christian, which must be displeasing to our Lord. Indeed, the greatest saints have always been the most conscious of their depravity. Nevertheless, we cannot use that fact to avoid the logic of the argument. How can we receive God's good gifts in answer to prayer, if we do not ask in accordance with his will? And how can we ask like that, unless we are obeying God's will already revealed in Scripture? So we take the astonishing, exciting possibility that verse 22 seems to hold out to us, that we will *receive from him anything we ask*, and rationalize our ordinary, often disappointing, experience by attributing it to our inability to obey God perfectly.

Our mistake is to make God's answers to prayer conditional on our obedience, whereas John's purpose is to fashion our asking on this pattern of obedience. On the one hand, clearly these great promises about prayer (see John 14:14, 16–23) do not give us carte blanche to get anything we want from God. This would make God indulgent, but hardly loving. On a merely human level, no parent gives a child everything the child wants, because the parent realizes what a spoiled, self-centred individual the child would become. Moreover, the child may demand things which would actually harm him or her, and love will say 'No'. If God were simply a supplier of our every wish or whim, which of us would dare ever to pray again? Like children, we often do not know what is best for us. But, on the other hand, prayer is not a sort of quid pro quo, by which God rewards us, answering our prayers according to what we have 'put in' and how pleased he is with us. Prayer is the expression of our requests to a loving, heavenly Father who loves both to hear and to answer his children, according to his wisdom as to what is best, or, as John puts it later in 5:14, 'according to his will'. Understood in this way, verse 22b becomes not so much an impossible challenge as an encouragement. As we seek to live in a way that pleases God, practising his truth and love, our desires become moulded to his. We want his will in our lives and the lives of others, rather than pursuing our own selfish desires willy-nilly. The more we enjoy and develop that relationship, as obedient children, the more we shall find ourselves asking for and receiving those things that are pleasing to God.

As a further encouragement, John takes those many commands we need to obey and combines all that pleases God into the one great statement of verse 23, with its two equally balanced, essential ingredients: *And this is his command: to believe in the name of his Son, Jesus Christ, and to love one another.* Here is John's irreducible minimum for Christian faith and experience. This verse provides both a summary of all his teaching and a fulcrum for the whole letter. The two central truths are here. The God who is light has revealed himself in the unchanging truth of his Word, written in the Scriptures, incarnate in the Son. Here alone is ultimate reality. The response that he requires is belief. The Greek verb for *to believe* is in an aorist tense indicating a definite action at a specific point in time. We believed. But the God who is love calls upon us to allow his love to flow into and through our lives, so that we become channels of that love to others, in all its practical help and self-giving sacrifice. So the verb for *to love* is in a continuous present tense; love is the constantly expressed evidence of that commitment of faith. Faith and love must go together.

But John is also concerned to define a little further what true believing is, perhaps with an eye particularly towards the gnostic teachers. In John's writing, the verb *pisteuō* (believe) used with the dative, as here, usually means 'believing that something is true, and so credible', rather than 'making a personal commitment to someone' (for which he usually uses *pisteuō eis*, believing into). Howard Marshall, who makes this point in his commentary, concludes:

> There is a certain stress here on the thought of right belief: the readers are to believe in the name of Jesus Christ, the Son of God, a stress that is demanded by the situation in which false beliefs about Jesus were prevalent. Belief in the name of Jesus means believing that his name contains the power which it signifies, so that the question is not simply one of right belief, but of trust in the one who is the object of the Christian confession.[1]

A true Christian, then, is one who obeys both the commands, to believe and to love. In this world, such responses will always be less than perfect and tainted with sin, but the continuance in them is the all-important mark of genuineness.

That is also the thrust of the last verse of this chapter. Spiritual life ('abiding in Christ') and obedience feed and reinforce each other. John is gathering together all the themes we have already explored with him about fellowship with God (1:6–7), in terms of remaining in Christ (2:24–28), through obedience to his commands (2:3–8). He underlines again that this is no vague super-spiritual notion, no empty mysticism, to which anyone might lay claim. It has content: belief (Jesus is the Son of God in human flesh) and behaviour (we are to love one another). What John adds here is the wonderful assurance that not only do we live in him, but he lives in us. This was exactly what the Lord Jesus himself promised: 'Anyone who loves me will obey my teaching. [Note again the two constituents of faith and love blended together.] My Father will

---

[1] Marshall, p. 201.

love them, and we will come to them and make our home with them'
(John 14:23).

That promise opens the way for John to share with us the ultimate
source of our knowledge, *the Spirit he gave us*. Knowledge of that sort will
not be shaken by the imaginative fantasies of the antichrists. Its source is
the Holy Spirit, given to us by the Father. Our knowledge and assurance
in the end come from God himself. So there is a marvellous blend of the
objective evidence and the subjective experience by which we may know
that we really do belong to God. The Holy Spirit takes the evidence of the
historical life, death and resurrection of the Word made flesh, in the pages
of the written Word of Scripture, and so awakens our minds to its truth
and our wills to its imperatives that we are brought to repent and to
believe the good news, as we confess that Jesus Christ is Lord. To this
John adds the objective evidence of a changed life, with a new concern to
live righteously in obedience to Christ's commands, and to reflect his
character not only by holiness but by a sincere love for God and for all
his people.

As we see these evidences within us, the Spirit himself assures us of the
genuineness of our Christianity, by his inner witness. 'The Spirit himself
testifies with our spirit that we are God's children' (Rom. 8:16). How good
it is to know that all this is the gift of God, in the Holy Spirit, from the
moment of our first awakening to spiritual realities, to the moment we see
him and are like him. With these resources we can live to please him. In
the words of John Newton, ''Tis grace has brought me safe thus far, / and
grace will lead me home.'[2]

---

[2] 'Amazing Grace', by John Newton (1725–1807).

1 John 4:1–6

13. Testing the spirits

Chapter 3 ended with the conviction that our ultimate assurance as Christians depends on, and is given by, the indwelling ministry of the Holy Spirit. But this raises another issue in John's thoughts as he continues his battle with the false teachers for the minds and hearts of the churches of Asia Minor. For many of those who had divided the churches were equally keen to appeal to the witness of the Spirit, in support of their false teaching and spurious claims. What is to be done when different theologies are being propounded by those who claim the same authority?

John's answer is *test the spirits* (1). For the world has never been without all sorts of fantastic religious notions and cults, and the truth of God's revelation has always been counterfeited by false prophets. The explosion of cultic activity and interest recently, especially on the fringes of the church, underlines that our generation is no exception to the rule. There are a few today who claim to be God, the perfect revelation of the deity for this time in history, and some apparently believe them. Within the church there are many who claim to speak directly as, or for, God. Their utterances may be prefaced by the formula 'Thus saith the Lord', or the approach may be less formal: 'I have a word from the Lord for you.' There are travelling prophets who claim to speak authoritatively to the nations, or (more often) to the church. There are those who claim the authority of God to direct others' lives, including decisions about work, or marriage, or where they live, by virtue of their direct communication with God. There are those who claim the power of God to exorcise or heal, or to perform signs and wonders. Any thinking Christian (and to be biblical we must be thinking!) will want to assess these claims to determine whether they are genuine or bogus. We are not called upon to be naive or gullible, fondly believing all who claim to speak for God. We must follow John's exhortation to test these phenomena, not cynically but lovingly, by applying the two key criteria laid down in this paragraph.

1. Examine what they say (4:1–3)

The imperative of verse 1 to test the spirits is very clear and strong and it is our responsibility to obey it. We are all impressed by the novel or the unusual, and it is tempting to ascribe all such phenomena to the power of God. But John specifically warns us not to believe all that we are told, but to discern its origin, whether it comes from God or not. *Because many false prophets have gone out into the world* we have to be on guard against the spurious. Such 'prophecies' or 'claims' may be unreal in the sense of being the delusions of people who are enormously enthusiastic and who really believe what they say. They are rather like those football supporters who make the most extravagant claims about the imminent successes of their mediocre teams. Events later prove them to have been deluded. Their claims are false. Or they could be the lies of those who are imposters, deliberately wanting to deceive others for their own personal benefit. False prophets may even produce evidence to 'prove' that what they say is real, but that is no guarantee that they are from God. Miraculous powers are no proof in themselves of the truth of those who exercise them. There were magicians in Egypt who could imitate some of the miraculous deeds God did through Moses (Exod. 7:22; 8:7; but see also 8:18–19). There was Simon, the Samaritan sorcerer, who had amazed people for a long time with his magic (Acts 8:11). Such signs are to be tested.

This is especially true of spoken prophecy which purports to be a word from God, and this is what John is especially concerned about here. It was no new problem for God's people. Back in Deuteronomy, through Moses, God addresses the same issue.

> You may say to yourselves, 'How can we know when a message has not been spoken by the Lord?' If what a prophet proclaims in the name of the Lord does not take place or come true, that is a message the Lord has not spoken. That prophet has spoken presumptuously.
> (Deut. 18:21–22)

It is a very useful test; but, of course, the problem is that it cannot be applied at the time the message is given. An earlier chapter emphasizes that the content of the message is the all-important factor.

> If a prophet, or one who foretells by dreams, appears among you and announces to you a sign or wonder, and if the sign or wonder spoken of takes place, and the prophet says, 'Let us follow other gods' (gods you have not known) 'and let us worship them,' you must not listen to the words of that prophet or dreamer. The Lord your God is testing you to find out whether you love him with all your heart and with all your soul. It is the Lord your God you must follow, and him you must revere . . . That prophet or dreamer must be put to death . . . You must purge the evil from among you.
> (Deut. 13:1–5)

It is a question of content. Does the message encourage God's people to worship and obey him, or does it lead them into idolatry? What the prophet says matters far more than how the prophet says it, or whatever apparently supernatural signs are produced to support it. The test is not whether it feels right, but whether it is true. And here the plumb line of God's revealed truth in the Scriptures must be applied. Every Christian has that solemn responsibility. John addresses all the church members, the *agapētoi*, not just the elders or overseers. We have to determine whether the message is from God. In doing this, we can be sure that the God who is eternal truth is not going to be contradicting what he has already said. John will apply God's word in verse 2, and so must we. Preachers will want to say often to their congregations, 'Do not believe it because I say it, but because God says it in his Word.' They will want to produce congregations of 'Bereans' who examine the Scriptures every day to see if what is said is true (see Acts 17:11). Any number of miraculous signs which may be adduced to support teaching contrary to the Bible cannot be from God, and therefore have no authority for the Christian.

Since it is the great work of the Holy Spirit to testify about Christ and exalt him (John 16:13–14), the person of the Lord Jesus becomes the touchstone of truth or error. When Paul wrote to the church in Corinth, he had a very simple test by which the true and false could be distinguished. 'No one who is speaking by the Spirit of God says, "Jesus be cursed," and no one can say, "Jesus is Lord," except by the Holy Spirit'

(1 Cor. 12:3). John is making the same point, though it is especially directed towards the denial of the incarnation, which was the cardinal gnostic heresy. As we have seen, they were prepared to believe that the Spirit came upon Jesus in a special way, but denied his pre-existence and therefore his full deity. Such a denial indicates the presence of the spirit of antichrist (3). So we are not to look for enlightenment or spiritual help from those who deny the deity of our Lord Jesus Christ, or his full humanity, whether they are academic theologians or Jehovah's Witnesses on the doorstep. If we are to be biblically positive about Christ, we have to be negative about error. This is not an incentive to indulge in theological witch-hunts, but to recognize where the Scriptures draw the lines between truth and error, and to draw them there ourselves. The spirit of antichrist is still abroad in the spirit of our age, with its mind set against allowing even for a moment that Christ's claims could be true. It manifests itself not only in the media boardrooms, but also in the councils of those Christian groups which refuse to affirm the truth of God's revelation in Scripture and therefore to identify its denial as heresy. Interestingly enough, the battle today is in the same key area, concerning the person of Christ. 'Who is this Jesus?' is not only the central question for evangelism, it is by virtue of that fact the central test of Christian orthodoxy. It is not the only test, but it is the most critical.

2. Look at how they live (4:4–6)

Because we have learned that belief and behaviour are always harnessed together, we are not surprised to find that John expands the way in which his test works out, by looking beyond the content of the false teaching to the effects it produces. Each of these three verses begins with a different pronoun, introducing a different group of people. *You* (4) refers to all Christians, *they* (5) to the non-Christian false prophets, and *we* (6) to the apostles and the true teachers who stand in the true apostolic succession.

At first sight verse 4 seems to be denied by common experience. How can John say that the Christians have overcome the false prophets, when they were proving an increasing threat to the health and existence of the church? Even more is this the case in our day when the mainline denominations are riddled with a radical theology which denies Christ and ridicules those who believe the Bible to be God's inerrant Word. But John is right, because the false teachers have not won the true believers over to their cause. The apostle himself stood firm and so did many of the believers who were strengthened by this letter. The same is true today. I like the way Gordon Clark puts it: 'We children of John have conquered the false prophets . . . We still believe in the virgin birth, the atonement and the resurrection. We have conquered them. They could not conquer us.'[1] By applying the test of truth, Christians remain true; their faith is not destroyed and their Saviour is not denied. He himself promised this when he said about his sheep, 'They will never follow a stranger; in fact, they will run away from him because they do not recognise a stranger's voice' (John 10:5). The antichristian wolf may come in sheep's clothing in order to ravage and disperse Christ's flock, but they cannot be overcome. Verse 4b explains why: *the one who is in you is greater than the one who is in the world.* Christ's sheep are united to the Shepherd, who is the Truth. They have no confidence in themselves, but they know that the cross and the empty tomb have proved their Shepherd's superior power over all his enemies. Moreover, because he is the Truth, those who fight against him fight against the structures of reality, and so they are doomed to fail. Besides this, power is available to each child of God as we remain in him and draw, by faith, upon his limitless resources. 'We are more than conquerors through him who loved us' (Rom. 8:37).

By contrast, the false teachers are tied to this world (5), the world which is passing away (2:17). The world is their origin and their audience. That is why so many of their heresies include the building of a new world order, a new government or a new system, usually with their leader as messiah at its head. The world of humanity in rebellion against God is attracted by the false prophets and their cults because fundamentally they have the same desires and inclinations. They will always get a hearing. When such 'prophets', political or religious, proclaim the glory of human beings and the fulfilment of human desires, at whatever cost and by any sort of behaviour, people will jump at the idea. We human beings want to be assured that we are basically all right, and that any ideas about sin and judgment or accountability to a creator God are outdated and unnecessary. There is an attraction in restating the Christian gospel in terms of an ethic, in changing the message from one of submission to the lordship of Jesus Christ to one of following his splendid example, or asking him to touch us up in those areas of our lives that need a fresh coat of paint. It is

---

[1] Clark, p. 127.

all governed by this world and the desire to make it a more comfortable place where you can enjoy yourself more. It has nothing to say on the issues of eternity. It has no dynamic by which lives can be changed, and offers no ultimate significance beyond the grave.

But the true apostles, equally, are known by what they teach (6). Their origin is God himself and their audience consists of those who know God. Now this of course is precisely what Cerinthus and his followers claimed for themselves – that they knew God. But John's point is that they indicate the emptiness of their claim by refusing to listen to the word of God in the apostolic teaching. The only way in which human beings can come to know God is by God choosing to reveal himself, perhaps by actions, but necessarily by words, by verbal propositions. The apostolic doctrine claims to be just such a revelation, and our attitude to it indicates whether we are governed by *the Spirit of truth* or *the spirit of falsehood*. The NIV translation gives a capital to the *Spirit of truth*, perhaps on the grounds that this title is given to the Holy Spirit in John's Gospel (14:17; 15:26; 16:13), but this does not seem necessary in the light of the plural 'spirits' in verse 1. It would be meaningless to talk about testing whether the Holy Spirit is from God. John's concern is with people who are active in the church, with how to distinguish pseudo-prophets from true teachers. We do not try to see into their hearts. That would be as impossible as it is unnecessary. We need to listen to what they say, what they are confessing about Christ, and then to observe who their followers are.

In our relativistic age, we constantly need to be reminded that some things are always true and others always false. Truth is not just the present consensus of opinion; it is defined by the character of God. Today's false prophets are just as persuasive and just as lethal as those of the first century. They will say the Bible has authority, but is not the supreme authority. They will affirm belief in the resurrection, but not that the body of Christ was actually raised on the third day. The spirit of falsehood is a spirit of deceit. It is only by receiving the apostles' teaching and living a life that accords with this truth that we can know God. We are not to accept substitutes.

1 John 4:7–12

14. Does God really love us?

The last three words of verse 8 form one of the most profound statements of the whole Bible and perhaps for many people today one of the hardest to believe. *God is love.* When we think of this 'grubby tennis ball' of a planet, set in the vast infinity of space, our own lives as just moments in the onward surge of time, and our individuality among countless millions, can we really talk meaningfully about God loving us? And when we look at the world with all its evil and suffering, so many damaged and broken lives, how can there be a God who really loves? Yet, John insists, this is the very nature of God. And if we are not to empty the word 'God' of all its meaning, we must realize that such an infinite yet personal Creator is not too great to be bothered with my tiny life. He is so great that he *can* be bothered with each of us individually.

Our study of the last few paragraphs has been rather like a progression through the anterooms in a great palace, each one more breathtaking as we move nearer to the throne room. We have seen the splendour of the King's magnificent provision for his children in the revolutionary difference of their attitudes and actions when compared with those of the world. We have marvelled at his detailed love and care for each one of us, accepting us in our weakness and producing confidence in our lives as we reflect his love. But now the magnificence becomes overwhelming as the throne-room doors are flung open and we are introduced to the glorious person who has done all this – the God who is love. Everything else in the splendour of these verses circles around this one supreme reality: 'God is love.'

John is not identifying a quality which God possesses; he is making a statement about the essence of God's being. It is not simply that God loves, but that he *is* love. We are helped to understand this when we remember that God is revealed in Scripture as the holy Trinity, three persons in one God. We shall never be able to comprehend the full meaning of this with our finite minds, but at least we can grasp that at the heart of the deity there is a dynamic interrelationship of love. Love flows between the three persons in a constant interaction, so that every activity expresses the love which is the divine nature. The Father loves the Son; the Son loves the Father; the Spirit loves the Son; and so on. This is not just a static description, but a living, active dynamism. God loves, within his own being, because his nature is to love. Therefore, to imagine that God does not love us is to deny his true nature, to repudiate his character. It is to distort the free grace of God into something much less worthy, a conditional 'love' that depends on the attractiveness or worthiness of the object for it to be exercised. Divine love (*agapē*) is utterly different. It cannot be earned; it cannot be deserved. God loves us because that is his nature.

This helps us to understand more clearly what John means when he affirms in verse 7 that *love comes from God*. He is as much its source as he is the source of all true light (1:5). This will underline why love for one another stands along with belief in Christ as the main criterion for proving that we have a true knowledge of God. It also helps us to interpret the second part of verse 7, *Everyone who loves has been born of God and knows God*. Clearly John is not teaching that every manifestation of human love is a sign of genuine spiritual life. Plummer argues, 'If God is the source of all love, then whatever love a man has in him comes from God; and this part of his moral nature is of Divine origin.'[1] While agreeing that the capacity to love is part of what is meant when we speak of men and women being made in the image of God, and that loving human relationships among non-Christian people are part of God's common grace, we must not confuse this with being born of God and knowing God. There is no doubt that in verse 7 John is talking about Christian love for the Christian community. The definite article before *love* in the Greek here particularizes that special quality of divine love which ought to characterize Christian fellowship. It is love for our fellow believers that John puts forward as irrefutable evidence of the new birth. Its absence, whatever a person's pretensions may be, indicates that he or she has no true personal knowledge of God (8a). John is also aware, however, that the word 'love' needs

---

[1] Plummer, p. 10.

definition and clarification, and so he focuses on two great evidences, in which the love of God can be both seen and communicated.

1. God's love is seen in the cross of Christ (4:9–10)

These two verses are packed full of meaning as John elaborates his second great theme. Since God is love, all our definitions of what love is and how it behaves must be drawn from him if they are to accord with reality. This also helps to elaborate and explain the quality of love, to which John has been referring in the previous two verses. The love which is the proof of a true relationship with God is a love which is manifested in actions for the benefit of others, even to the point of self-sacrifice. To understand that love we have to understand the heart of God himself.

We have already seen that the action of Jesus in laying down his life for his people is the perfect demonstration of divine love (3:16). Now, as John returns to the theme of the cross again, he begins by looking at its meaning from God's viewpoint. *This is how God showed his love among us.* The verb (*phaneroō*) was used back at the start of the letter (1:2) to describe the coming of Christ, the life, into the world. Here the death of Jesus is seen as the public appearance of God's love for his people. *Among us* is literally 'in us', which Clark suggests might be better translated 'in our case'.[2] Let us also note at this point the important clause in verse 10a, *not that we loved God*. This is no reciprocation by God, meeting people halfway because they have shown some desire to be right with their master. The initiative is entirely God's. He decides to manifest his love to those who do not love him and who do not want to love him, to enemies and rebels armed to the teeth against him, to a world of lost sinners. Let us acknowledge once and for all that if it were not for the fact that God is love, we would have no expectation of mercy or forgiveness, no hope and no future. The initiative in the work of our salvation belongs entirely to the God of love.

From verses 9 and 10 we can build up the full picture John wants to give us of this loving God in action. *He sent his one and only Son* (9). The object is placed emphatically at the beginning and then the subject and verb are reversed, so, to quote Lenski, a more accurate rendering of the feeling of the original would be '*his Son* he has sent, *God* has sent'.[3] To increase the

---

2 Clark, p. 134.
3 Lenski, p. 501.

emphasis on the amazing fact that God should bother with human beings, the word 'God' is repeated over and over again in this paragraph.

The adjective 'only begotten' (*monogenēs*) is added to the description of the Son who came. We are familiar with its use in John 3:16. The NIV translation *one and only* catches the meaning well. It means 'unique, one of a kind'. It was amazing that God should send a Son, but to send his *only* Son is a measure of the magnitude of this love. The same word is used of Isaac in Hebrews 11:17, to illustrate the greatness of Abraham's faith and obedience when God tested him. He was prepared to sacrifice his one and only son, the son who had been promised so long, if that was what Yahweh commanded. We have here the idea of a Son who is specially precious and greatly loved because he is the only one. God had only one Son, and he was sent into a hostile environment, into a rebel world, on a rescue mission to redeem us and reconcile us to God. *This is love.*

But there is more, for the precious, only Son was sent *as an atoning sacrifice for our sins.* The word is *hilasmos*, on which we commented at 2:2. Love finds the means by which just and righteous wrath can be satisfied and so turned away, in order that forgiveness may be offered and reconciliation achieved. The only way was at infinite cost to the one who loves. 'The depth of God's love is to be seen precisely in the way in which it bears the wounds inflicted on it by mankind and offers full and free pardon.'[4] It is no help to our understanding to pretend that a loving God would not require an atoning sacrifice, because he would not punish sin. This would be to destroy the truth that God is light and to remove all grounds of morality. The nobler, biblical way is to magnify the love of God by seeing at what tremendous cost the atonement was made, and therefore of what amazing length, devotion and scope this love is capable. It also underlines the fact that only those who have been ransomed by that love know its full extent. 'Even angels long to look into these things' (1 Pet. 1:12).

> Stronger his love than death or hell;
> Its riches are unsearchable;
> The firstborn sons of light
> Desire in vain its depths to see;
> They cannot reach the mystery,
> The length, and breadth, and height.[5]

---

[4] Marshall, p. 215.
[5] 'O Love Divine, How Sweet Thou Art', by Charles Wesley (1707–88).

Finally, let us grasp a further truth about what the death of Christ accomplished. He died *for our sins.* It was because of our sins that Jesus died, for he had none of his own. In that death he dealt with them, because he paid the penalty of separation from the heavenly Father, which we deserve. Our sins are therefore forgiven and removed because of the cross, the consequence being *that we might live through him* (9b). So the ultimate purpose of this sending and commissioning was that we might receive eternal life in the place of certain death. It is only through Jesus that such life can come to us. He is the personal mediator who pleads for us at the Father's throne (2:1). He is the source and the channel of spiritual, eternal life. Not only are the rebels pardoned; they are made sons and daughters. And 'a son belongs to [the family] for ever' (John 8:35). This is love. Its source is in God; it is manifest in the person and work of the Lord Jesus Christ; its purpose is the blessing of a multitude of lives, made right with God, through the death of his Son.

2. God's love is seen in how Christians love one another (4:11–12)

Verse 11 calls not so much for comment as for grateful obedient implementation. Repeating the exhortation of verse 7 with which the section begins, 'let us love one another', John has now immensely strengthened his case and his readers' motivation. Note the little adverb *so* in the phrase *since God so loved us.* This takes us back to all the details of the preceding verses, and is intended as a further refutation of Cerinthus and his heresies. The one who suffered was the eternal, unique Son of the Father. It was his blood that flowed for our forgiveness. And those who have been forgiven will demonstrate this revolutionary change at the heart of their lives by a new love for one another. God's love supplies both the reason and the resources. If we are truly his children we shall want to be like our Father. But there is also a dimension of obligation in the verb. This is not just an extra ingredient that we might add to our discipleship if we feel especially moved to do so. We owe it to the loving Father not to slander his name any further by denying his love in our human relationships. If we have been cleansed through Christ's blood, our new lives must be clean, like his, as we mix with others in God's family. If we have appreciated something of the infinite price paid for our redemption, then we shall see at once how vital it is that we do not continue to indulge ourselves in sin. There is a new constraint within us that longs to live differently (Rom. 5:5). So the Christian church should be a community of love, unlike any other human society. It is true, as has been said, that the church exists for those who are not yet members, but it is also true that the love among her members should be one of her most powerful magnets.

This is the thought to which John moves us in verse 12, where the love between Christians is explicitly stated to reveal the love of God. It is an integral part of the witness of the church in the world to the reality of the gospel and the love of her Lord. *No one has ever seen God* is a statement almost exactly paralleled by John in the prologue to the Gospel (John 1:18). There it is the incarnation of Jesus which is thought of as the visible manifestation of the invisible God. Here it is the love between Christians. That in itself should make us stop and think about how important this responsibility is. If the church is the body of Christ on earth, then she must reflect his character in her relationships and inner life. The supernatural love of God for sinners like us has often been made more credible when unbelievers have seen it reflected in the lives of his children. Francis Schaeffer rightly described such love as 'the ultimate apologetic',[6] for the Lord himself said, 'Everyone will know that you are my disciples, if you love one another' (John 13:35). Love is the hallmark, the family characteristic. People should be able to see Christ's love in our fellowships. Isn't that the meaning, at least in part, of John's vision in the opening of the book of Revelation? He sees the risen Lord in all his splendour and glory 'among the lampstands' (Rev. 1:13), which we are later told represent the churches (Rev. 1:20) – in all likelihood the very churches to which this letter is addressed. The same message is being reinforced. Christ's physical presence is no longer with us in this world, but if people want to see Jesus, they should be able to meet him in the churches. They should encounter his love in the love we Christians have for one another. And again that means not just mystical visions, or wonderful warming words, but practical down-to-earth actions, the modern equivalent of washing one another's feet (John 13:14–17). Only then does God's love take its fullest effect in our lives. As we love one another, the life of God is manifest in us and continues to grow. It is also true that as we experience more of the indwelling life of God the Holy Spirit within us, we shall love our fellow

---

6 Francis Schaeffer, *The Church Before the Watching World* (Inter-Varsity Press, 1972).

believers more fervently and more practically than ever before. So God's love finds its completion by creating in us that same kind of self-giving love as his. It is a love that will send us into the world, as it sent his one and only Son, 'to give and not to count the cost'. It is a love that the hard-nosed cynicism of our society desperately needs to see, because it is the nearest many people will ever get to seeing the invisible God. The responsibility belongs to God's forgiven people. The church is his audiovisual presentation to a dying culture. People should be able to look at a Christian fellowship and see the God of love within his people. That is the goal God's love is working for, and for us to be content with anything less is to deny the gospel. If we know that God really loves us, let us allow that love to flow into and overflow from our lives. *Dear friends . . . we also ought to love one another.*

1 John 4:13–21

15. Grounds of assurance

In the early days of radio in the UK, George Bernard Shaw was giving a talk about the peculiarities of the English language, in the course of which he mentioned that there are only two words in English which begin with the sound 'sh' but are not spelt 'sh'. One listener wrote in to say that this seemed untrue. There was only one such word – 'sugar'. She received a postcard, in reply, on which there was just one sentence: 'Madam, are you sure?' Being sure is a perilous business, and nowhere more so than in matters of spiritual life, and yet John insists that God wants us to know that we are his and that our Christian experience is real.

At the heart of Christian assurance lies the conviction, with which the last section ended and which John repeats here in verses 13, 15 and 16, that 'we live in God and he in us'. We have all sorts of problems with a concept like that, in a culture where we are accustomed to judging the reality of everything by our senses. We cannot see this God (12a) because he is a spirit (John 4:24). He is not a collection of sensory data to be discovered and analysed, but an infinite, eternal person. Our feelings are an equally untrustworthy guide because they are notoriously subjective and easily deluded. The maxim that 'if it feels right, it is right' is no solid foundation for spiritual reality. All the normal methods we would apply in a quest for certainty seem irrelevant. So how *can* we be sure? In the next few verses, John presents five pieces of evidence.

1. We have received the Holy Spirit (4:13)

This takes up and reiterates the evidence which was last mentioned in 3:24. The difference is that there John affirmed that God gave us the Spirit, whereas here he says that God *has given us of his Spirit*. We should not, of course, be misled by this into thinking that John is withdrawing anything of what he has earlier stated, by indicating that the Holy Spirit is divisible into parts. This is the same mistake as thinking of the fullness of the Spirit as somehow getting more of the Spirit into us than we have, as though we could receive him by instalments. He is a person, one and indivisible; though we must also observe that the fact that he indwells one Christian does not mean that he cannot equally indwell all. So it is impossible for one to have 60% of the Spirit, but not at all impossible that he has less than all of us.

When first we are born again we receive the Holy Spirit, the life of God within. This is the uniform New Testament teaching from the day of Pentecost onwards. On that day Peter affirmed,

> Repent and be baptised, every one of you, in the name of Jesus Christ for the forgiveness of your sins. And you will receive the gift of the Holy Spirit. The promise is for you and your children and for all who are far off – for all whom the Lord our God will call.
> (Acts 2:38–39)

Paul can therefore teach that 'if anyone does not have the Spirit of Christ, they do not belong to Christ' (Rom. 8:9), the corollary being equally true. The greatest gift of the ascended Christ to his church on earth is the Holy Spirit, who is himself the source of all the other gifts and graces which we need in order to live consistently as God's children in this world. Being 'filled with the Spirit' (Eph. 5:18) must therefore be understood as being constantly energized and directed by the life of God within, as we open every area of our lives to his dynamic influence. It is the Spirit who produces the love of God in us towards our fellow Christians, as he works in all sorts of other ways also to make us like Christ. Because God is love, wherever his Spirit is active the evidence will be seen in love.

The living God within his people will always produce the characteristics of his life – holiness and righteousness, mercy and love. When believers experience that inner constraint to love others unselfishly, whereas before they might have feared, ignored or rejected them, that is evidence that the Holy Spirit is at work within them. It is a real assurance of salvation. But we must not avoid the negative implications too. Where someone claims to be a Christian but has no time for fellowship with others, criticizing the church and writing it off, practising a solitary devotion, do we not have to ask whether that person is deluded and whether God really does indwell him or her? Where the life of God is at work, it sweetens bitterness, melts hardness and multiplies love.

2. We have the apostolic testimony (4:14)

Linked to the witness of the Holy Spirit is the witness of the apostles. The one empowered the other, yet both were needed. The Lord Jesus himself taught his disciples this, bringing the two strands of testimony together.

> When the Advocate comes, whom I will send to you from the Father – the Spirit of truth who goes out from the Father – he will testify about me. And you also must testify, for you have been with me from the beginning.
> (John 15:26–27)

The *we* in this verse clearly refers to the apostolic company, as it did at the start of the letter. It was their unique privilege and responsibility to witness to what they saw and heard. Indeed, it is widely accepted that to have seen and been commissioned by the risen Lord was the ultimate test of New Testament apostleship. Others might be specially 'sent ones' (*apostoloi*), commissioned to specific tasks in the Christian community, as missionaries, for example, but the original eleven with the addition of Matthias (Acts 1:26), James the Lord's brother (Gal. 1:19) and Paul stand in a class apart. Interestingly, when Paul is defending his own authenticity as a true apostle of Christ he adduces as evidence the fact that he has 'seen Jesus our Lord' (1 Cor. 9:1). Our assurance therefore finds root in their testimony. We have not seen the Lord Jesus, but they did. They saw the eternal Word made flesh, in time and space in Jesus. As Peter confirms, 'We did not follow cleverly devised stories when we told you about the coming of our Lord Jesus Christ in power, but we were eye-witnesses of his majesty' (2 Pet. 1:16).

Note again how John compresses so much of what we have already learned into one short sentence. Resolutely he hammers the nails into the coffin of Gnosticism, again and again. The pre-existent Son was *sent* by the Father into *the world*. He came to be its Saviour by his real human death on the cross. These are the facts of the matter. The witness of the Spirit and the apostolic testimony belong together, for there can be no separation between the Spirit and the Word. The one who wrote the Word, inspiring its human authors, uses his specially designed tool to bring us to life and to build us up in the faith. The vindication of the reality of the Spirit's work in our lives is seen in commitment to the revelation of God, in the Scriptures.

3. We have personally acknowledged Jesus as God's Son (4:15)

Here again we recognize John's blend of truth and love, as we put this verse alongside verse 12. The emphasis this time is on the outward confession of the inner conviction. Only by faith in Jesus as the Son of God can an individual be joined to God in fellowship. Our relationship with God therefore depends upon a historical incarnation, namely that *Jesus is the Son of God.*

Clearly, John means more by 'acknowledgment' than simple intellectual acceptance of a fact of history; but today we have to stress that neither is it any less than that. Saving faith depends not just on a general warmth and positive feeling towards Christ, whatever some evangelistic presentations may imply. It depends on a doctrinal confession concerning the person of Christ, on which the whole of our experience of God actually depends. And further, the mark of that reality is a life which expresses personal faith in Christ as God, by obedience to his commands and growth in character like his. Neither of the two strands of truth and love is optional. They cannot be separated. This was why the creeds were formulated. The church knew that its members must be instructed and encouraged in right believing, which is not a matter of the mind alone, but a commitment of the will and the heart. We need to remind ourselves of that in a day when creeds or doctrinal bases are all too often dismissed as unacceptably restrictive and inhibiting, when some Christians refuse to sign their name to any statement of faith because 'God may tell us to believe something different tomorrow.' Any personal relationship we may claim to have with God has to be rooted in his revealed truth if it is to be assessed as genuine and not just wishful thinking.

Let us rejoice when we can affirm with the saints of the ages, from our heart, with a clear mind and a committed will,

I believe . . . in one Lord Jesus Christ, the only-begotten Son of God,
begotten of his Father before all worlds, God of God, Light of Light, very
God of very God, begotten, not made, being of one substance with the
Father, by whom all things were made: who for us men and for our
salvation came down from heaven, and was incarnate by the Holy
Ghost of the Virgin Mary, and was made man . . .[1]

It is a ground of assurance.

4. We have confidence in God's love (4:16–19)

Theological knowledge and doctrinal convictions are proved by living
experience, and deepened by it too. When a man and a woman pledge
themselves in a marriage service to live together as husband and wife, the
vows which they exchange include solemn promises that they can be
relied upon, whatever may happen. 'For better, for worse; for richer, for
poorer; in sickness and in health.' This is an expression of the love which
they already have for each other, which will deepen as they experience its
reality in practice through all the changing circumstances of life. Real love
can be relied on, but only a commitment of faith will prove it.

Our experience of God's love is very much like this. Because it is
grounded in his unchanging character (*God is love*), as we live in a daily
relationship of trust and obedience with him we are constantly in touch
with that divine love and learn to rely on it more and more (16). The verb
translated *rely* in the NIV more literally means 'believed', the perfect tense
implying an action which is still effective (which is presumably why the
NIV chooses to translate in the present tense). A couple who have been
happily married for some years often have such extensive areas of
agreement and mutual understanding that each can tell what the other is
thinking without any words being spoken. That sort of intimacy with God
is possible only if we rely on his love and live in him. If we would think his
thoughts, we must give ourselves to the study of his Word. If we would
experience more of his love, we must rely on him more thoroughly.
Sometimes we go through trials and testings for that very reason, because
the God who loves us wants us to rely on him more completely or to trust
him more fully. He allows such experiences to refine and strengthen our

---

[1] The Nicene Creed.

trust and to increase our appetite for him, for we never have less of Christ than we really desire.

At verse 17, John echoes the theme touched on at the end of verse 12, namely that God's love is always looking for and working towards completeness. Because he is perfection himself, how can our loving Father be satisfied with anything less for his children? 'He who began a good work in you will carry it on to completion until the day of Christ Jesus' was Paul's encouragement to the Philippians (Phil. 1:6). In verse 12 John's emphasis was on God's love being seen in the love Christians have for one another, whereas here the perspective is forward-looking, to the purpose of this work in its completion, which is *confidence on the day of judgment*. The thought that ties the two verses together is that the more we grow to be like Jesus, the more God's love is perfected in our lives. And this is no impossible dream, because *in this world we are like Jesus*. Even though we are on earth and he is in heaven, in his grace and love God has given us the privilege of sharing some foretastes of that inheritance which will be fully ours only when we see him. We are already 'blessed in the heavenly realms with every spiritual blessing in Christ' (Eph. 1:3). We already know Christ as our wisdom, righteousness, holiness and redemption (1 Cor. 1:30). Christ is our life (Col. 3:4) already in this world. 'The Spirit himself testifies with our spirit that we are God's children. Now if we are children, then we are heirs – heirs of God and co-heirs with Christ' (Rom. 8:16–17). The love that God lavishes upon us his adopted children (3:1) is the same love with which he loves the only begotten Son. So, if all this is ours now, by grace, we do not need to fear the judgment day.

Fear and *love* are mutually exclusive (18a). If we are afraid that God is going to punish us, we cannot yet be aware of the fullness of his everlasting love. Often the problem is that we transfer the model of parenthood derived from our experience as children directly on to God. If our parents withheld love as a means of conditioning or disciplining us, or if we never had the security of knowing that nothing could shake their love, we can easily regard God with a mixture of fear and gratitude, always wondering when the blow will fall. But that is not love. How many Christians are caught up in this web of fear! Often they are the most sensitive and lonely people, but they live in the anticipation of some calamity being visited upon them as judgment for their past sins, or retribution for not making more progress in holy living. The result is usually paralysis. They imagine that God is waiting with a big stick to beat them every time they fail. They precondition themselves to do just that. Not surprisingly, the devil is all too ready to pile in with his accusations and whisper that they cannot expect God to spend any more time on such hopeless, useless specimens. Perhaps they are not really Christians at all!

But the God who is love wants his children to have confidence. Look back again to 3:1–2 and drink it in! We can have complete confidence in Jesus, God's Son. Because he shed his blood for our forgiveness, we can call God 'Father', and know that we are fully accepted for the sake of his beloved Son. *Punishment* is quite foreign to someone who is forgiven and loved. So, as the Amplified Bible Classic Edition beautifully expresses it, the perfect love of God in Christ 'turns fear out of doors and expels every trace of terror'. When we are in Christ, we are as he is. Does the Lord Jesus cringe in terror before the Father? Of course not. Then, humbly but sincerely, we may share his boldness, his confidence and freedom of speech. He has loved us with an everlasting love (Jer. 31:3), which will never let us down and never let us go. If we are always afraid of what our Father may do to us, we do not really love him, and if we do not love him it is because we do not really believe that he loves us.

Although the AV translates verse 19 'We love him, because he first loved us', textual evidence has established that the 'him' was a later addition by editors who thought the verb needed a specific object. The NIV, in common with other modern translations, simply affirms, *We love because he first loved us.* In making a new paragraph at this point, the NIV translators link the thought to the love of Christians for their brothers and sisters, which will follow in the next two verses. Indeed, John is stressing that the proof of the genuineness of any claim to love God is love for his visible children. But here we are brought to realize that to claim a real love for God and for others is not in itself presumption, because it is a response to his initiative. In fact, it is possible only because of God's love, in the first place. That is what we need to grasp. God loved us enough to send the Lord Jesus to die for our sins, so the punishment has already been met in full; there is nothing left to pay. He did it for me! And when that grips me in the depths of my being, how can I but respond in love? What we discover is that the more we love him, and demonstrate that reality by loving our fellow Christians, however weakly and faintly, the less we are a prey to fear. Fear is the child of bondage. Love is the child of freedom. 'So if the Son sets you free, you will be free indeed' (John 8:36).

5. We love our brothers and sisters (4:20–21)

This final ground of assurance brings us full circle back to 4:7, where this major section began. When God's love begins to fill our lives, he not only gives us a model of how we should live in our human relationships, but he gives us both the desire and the ability to begin to do it; to reflect his love to others. Once again John reminds us of this most practical of all his tests of Christian reality. It is the easiest thing in the world to make a verbal profession of Christian commitment, or to say 'I love God.' But if we do not at the same time love our brother and sister, it is a lie. Love for the unseen Lord is best expressed not just in words, but in deeds of love towards the Lord's people whom we do see.

Is this not one of our greatest sins as Christians today? We may talk a lot about loving God, we may express it in our worship with great emotion, but what does it mean when we are so critical of other Christians, so ready to jump to negative conclusions about people, so slow to bear their burdens, so unwilling to step into their shoes? Such lovelessness totally contradicts what we profess and flagrantly disobeys God's commands. It becomes a major stumbling block to those who are seeking Christ and renders any attempts at evangelism useless. In many churches and fellowships we need a fresh repentance on this matter, a new humbling before God, an honest confession of our need and a cry to God for mercy and grace to change us.

Let us not avoid the plain teaching of Scripture. If we do not love those fellow Christians whom we know well and see regularly within our fellowship circles, we *cannot* be loving God. We may have occasional warm feelings, but these can be merely sentimental and unrelated to other people in their real-life situations. The proof of true love is not emotion or words, but deeds, which reach out to help others in need. But the other side of the coin is that such practical caring love can be a wonderful ground of assurance. There is a divine obligation laid upon us all in verse 21. The whole law is summed up in the royal law of love and we cannot love God without keeping his commandments. His will is that we should reflect the image of our Creator, who is love, by our love for one another. Plummer quotes the words of Pascal: 'We must know men in order to love them, but we must love God in order to know him.'[2] That is true, but John would insist that we add, *anyone who loves God must also love their brother and sister.*

---

[2] Plummer, p. 109.

1 John 5:1–5

16. Faith – the key to victory

As we have been climbing the staircase of Christian reality with the apostle John, we have become used to certain familiar themes and favourite subjects. Although perspectives are constantly changing, we have seen how the great themes of truth and love, belief and behaviour, blend together, over and over again. This fifth and final chapter of the letter will prove to be no exception, especially as John moves towards his great disclosure of the motivation and purpose which have governed his aim in writing. 'I write these things to you who believe in the name of the Son of God so that you may know that you have eternal life' (5:13). But here, in the opening paragraph, John introduces us to a new term, *faith* (*pistis*). Strange though it may seem, the noun is found nowhere else in the letter, or indeed in John's Gospel, although the verbal form, translated 'believe' (*pisteuō*), is used several times.

These verses concentrate on the nature of Christian faith and its evidences in the life of the one who believes, but they are not unrelated to the grounds of assurance John has been expounding in chapter 4, and especially to the necessity of love. Indeed, verse 1 joins the two great ingredients of New Testament Christianity, faith and love, together. As soon as John has defined the core belief *that Jesus is the Christ* as the means by which the new birth is brought about (1a), he immediately moves into the inevitable expression and proof of faith's existence and genuineness: love for God and for his children (1b). To the apostle these two constituents of Christian reality are as inseparable as two sides of the same coin. Faith that does not lead to love is meaningless. Love that is not based on faith is powerless.

Neither is John alone in making this spiritual equation. Readers of Paul's New Testament letters will be familiar with the apostolic criteria which he constantly applies to the reality of the Christian profession of the churches to which he writes. 'Ever since I heard about your faith in the Lord Jesus and your love for all God's people, I have not stopped giving thanks for you, remembering you in my prayers' (Eph. 1:15–16). To the Colossians he writes, 'We always thank God, the Father of our Lord Jesus Christ, when we pray for you, because we have heard of your faith in Christ Jesus and of the love you have for all God's people' (Col. 1:3–4). Or again, to the Thessalonians: 'We remember before our God and Father your work produced by faith, your labour prompted by love, and your endurance inspired by hope in our Lord Jesus Christ' (1 Thess. 1:3). And for good measure, Peter addresses exactly the same marks of reality in writing to the scattered congregation of Asia Minor: 'Though you have not seen him [Christ], you love him; and even though you do not see him now, you believe in him and are filled with an inexpressible and glorious joy' (1 Pet. 1:8). For New Testament Christians neither faith nor love was an optional extra; they were the twin pillars on which all true Christian experience rested.

1. The nature of faith

Once again John uses the phrase *Everyone who* does such-and-such, as he has done on several previous occasions in the letter (see 2:29; 3:3–4; 4:2–3, 7). It is a phrase that includes all who satisfy the given condition (in this case, all who believe *that Jesus is the Christ*), and excludes everyone else. It is designed both to increase the assurance of the true Christian and to exclude all those who would try to climb into the sheep pen some other way than by entering through the only door, which is Christ (John 10:1–9).

As always, the Bible's emphasis is on the object of faith, not the subjective experience of believing. In our existentialist culture, we find that very hard to accept. There is a widespread distrust of what used to be called 'historical facts'. How can we know anything, with certainty, about the past? We can only look through our own culturally tinted spectacles and put an interpretative gloss on the people and events we think we perceive. We can only believe certain propositions to be true as a personal act of faith: 'This view of things makes sense for me and therefore pleases me.' Or so it is claimed. Of course, this runs in parallel with the idea that there are no moral absolutes existing independently of ourselves. They can exist only if we allow them to exist, in our own minds; and while that may be fine for one individual, it does not necessarily have any compulsion, or even relevance, for another individual. There is nothing either good or bad, but thinking makes it so.

In such a situation, I may be free to believe what I like and to behave how I wish, within a wide framework of tolerance, but I am not free to require you to believe what I believe. I cannot say to you, 'This is Truth,' since there is no longer any moral concept that can compel belief. So we are left simply with the experience of believing – anything or nothing, as the whim may take us. And if there is no ultimate content in which to believe (neither a 'someone' nor even a 'something'), then all we have left with which to give meaning to life is our subjective experience of believing whatever we like. Over a hundred years ago, Robert Louis Stevenson foreshadowed this attitude when he said, 'To travel hopefully is a better thing than to arrive.' The journey is everything, because there can no longer be a destination.

This is the cultural vacuum into which John's unequivocal statement has still to be spoken. Sometimes we come across people who say, 'I wish I could have a faith.' Its content does not matter to them. They are true children of their culture. They are looking for an experience, any experience, to give some meaning and authenticity to their existence. But it is not 'faith' as an abstract idea that interests the New Testament writers. *Our faith* (4b), that is, Christian faith, has a distinctive and irreducible content. Put together the first part of verse 1 and the last part of verse 5 and we see what it is. Christians believe *that Jesus is the Christ, the Son of God*. That is not just an article of faith, it is *the* faith. It is this alone that makes a person a Christian. We need to be perfectly clear that whatever else people may claim to believe or whatever other positions they may hold, if they do not believe that Jesus is the Son of God they cannot have been born of God and cannot be called Christians.

From the very beginning of the church on the day of Pentecost, this was the content of the apostolic faith and gospel message: 'God has made this Jesus, whom you crucified, both Lord and Messiah' (Acts 2:36). It would be difficult to improve on Plummer's concise summary of the implications:

> To believe that Jesus is the Christ is to believe that One who was known as a man fulfilled a known and Divine commission; that He who was born

and was crucified is the Anointed, the Messiah of Israel, the Saviour of the world. To believe this is to accept both the Old and the New Testaments; it is to believe that Jesus is what He claimed to be, One who is equal with the Father, and as such demands of every believer the absolute surrender of self to Him.[1]

Throughout the letter John has been expounding for us just what he means. To believe in Christ is to believe in his deity (1:1–3), in the power of his death to cleanse from all sin (1:7) and to avert the righteous wrath of a holy God (2:2). It means that we believe that the love of God is expressed in its fullest measure by the cross of Christ (4:9–10), and that eternal life is experienced only by a faith-union with him, which is the product of his grace, appropriated by faith (5:11–12).

But the tenses used in verse 1a are also important, and particularly as we face the challenge of proclaiming the historical Jesus, who is the Christ of faith, to a generation whose only certainty is that if you are sure of anything then you are certainly wrong. John's view of faith is not believing against hope, but exercising faith so that we know we have eternal life. Is that really possible today? Verse 1 tells us that the person who *believes* (present tense) has been *born of God* (perfect – past – tense). Clearly, John is using the past tense to indicate something that is a present and continuing reality to the Christian. But surely there is more to it than that. He is also stating that when a person believes that Jesus is the Christ, he or she has been born again. On this reading, it is God who takes the initiative in the new birth, or the work of salvation, faith being both his gift and the first active sign of the new life, as the new Christian confesses that Jesus is the Christ.

This would certainly seem to accord with Paul's teaching in Ephesians 2. Having expounded our total inability to save ourselves because we are dead in transgressions and sins (1–3), Paul asserts, 'But . . . God . . . made us alive with Christ even when we were dead in transgressions . . . it is by grace you have been saved, through faith – and this is not from yourselves, it is the gift of God' (4–5, 8). If this is so, then salvation is indeed God's work from the very beginning. So, while we continue to preach the apostolic gospel and to present the apostolic challenge (repent and believe) to our faithless and unbelieving generation, we do so fully aware that we

---

[1] Plummer, p. 110.

are speaking to the spiritually dead, as we ourselves once were. We are not calling upon our hearers to summon up their natural human abilities so that they may believe in Christ, in order to be born of God. It is only God who can give life.

One of the clearest illustrations of this is in John's account of Jesus' raising of Lazarus, in chapter 11 of his Gospel. The man who had been four days in the tomb came out in response to a command from the Lord Jesus. 'Jesus called in a loud voice, "Lazarus, come out!"' (John 11:43). On the face of it nothing could be more foolish. How could a dead man hear the loudest voice? But then how could a spiritually dead person respond to the gospel command to repent and believe? The answer lies in the power of the one who spoke and in the executive authority of his word. Just as God created light with a word (Gen. 1:3), so he recreates spiritual life, he brings the dead sinner to birth, by his word of power. It is the life-giving word which raises the spiritually dead, and the first evidence of that having happened is that we believe that Jesus is the Christ.

That is why the Bible asserts that the Word of truth, the gospel, is always the agent of the new life. So Paul instructs the Romans, 'Faith comes from hearing the message, and the message is heard through the word about Christ' (Rom. 10:17). It is as the message that Jesus is the Son of God is faithfully presented that God regenerates and grants the gift of saving faith. For as Jesus himself said, 'Very truly I tell you, a time is coming and has now come when the dead will hear the voice of the Son of God and those who hear will live' (John 5:25). Charles Wesley sums it up with his customary perception:

> He speaks, and, listening to his voice,
> New life the dead receive;
> The mournful, broken hearts rejoice;
> The humble poor believe.[2]

So we do not need to fear for the gospel, whatever the prevailing cultural climate may be. God will still regenerate sinners wherever the message is proclaimed, and will still give to those who believe in his name the right to become children of God, born of God (John 1:12–13).

---

[2] 'O for a Thousand Tongues to Sing', by Charles Wesley (1707–88).

2. The effects of faith

If we rightly understand faith in Jesus to be a sign of the new birth, then the evidences of faith which John now goes on to enumerate are similarly confirmation of that new relationship which exists between the newborn child of God and the heavenly Father. There are three ways in which faith's reality is demonstrated in a Christian's life.

a. Love

As soon as we realize what has happened to us through the new birth, our response is one of gratitude and *love* to God. He has now become our Father; we are members of a new family. At the ordinary human level it is true that we have a special affection for, and interest in, the children of our friends. Therefore, we express our gratitude to the heavenly Father for all that he has done for us, by our own love for all of his children. This will apply first to our love for the only begotten Son, the Lord Jesus, but also to all of God's adopted *children*, as verse 2a makes clear. Since this is set in the context of the new family life, we are in fact proving our membership of that new unity by sincerely loving our new brothers and sisters. For without love of the brother or sister whom we have seen, any claim to love the invisible Father is a lie (4:20). In chapter 4 we were taught that love for our fellow Christians is part of our love for and obedience to God, while here it is shown to flow from that prior and dominating love relationship. What we are to learn is that neither one of these aspects of our love can exist without the other. Those who walk in the light with God have fellowship with one another (1:7).

Again, it is important to remember that John is not enjoining a duty upon Christians which we ought to strive to fulfil; rather he is describing a characteristic of real Christianity, without which no-one can claim to be truly regenerate. There is a third strand, to which we shall turn in a moment, and that is obedience (2b), but before we examine that in more detail it may be helpful to see how these three evidences of faith may work together in practice, to give us biblical assurance as Christians.

The more introspective we are by nature the greater may be our problem with assurance. We shall be particularly aware of the scriptural warnings against falling away, such as Hebrews 6:1–6 and 2 Corinthians 13:5. Many sensitive Christians seem to suffer agonies of doubt in these areas and even come to wonder whether they can ever be sure of their salvation. This very letter, of course, has applied a number of tests by which true believers can know that their faith is not a delusion. But all too often, instead of applying the objective criteria of Scripture, we find ourselves sinking into a slough of self-analysis, where our own subjective feelings (or lack of them) tyrannize us into thinking we cannot be truly Christ's. In such a condition we take evidences such as love for God and for our fellow believers, seen in obedience to his commands, and try to use them as a stick to beat ourselves into becoming better Christians. We do not feel sufficient love for others, perhaps, and so we begin to doubt whether we are really born again. But verse 2 provides a very practical corrective. It asks us, 'Do you love God? Are you seeking to obey his commands?' For if these qualities are present, we can know that our love for other Christians is genuine, whatever feelings we may or may not have.

Let us take the concrete example contained in the commandment 'You shall not give false testimony against your neighbour' (Exod. 20:16). We show our love to God by recognizing that this command reflects his truthful, loving character, and by keeping it. In so doing, we also love our neighbour by preserving him or her from lies which would destroy our neighbour's character or reputation. All three belong together – love for God, love for our brother or sister and obedience – as the outworking of the faith that says, 'God is truth and his way is best.' We can go forward, on that basis, with assurance.

b. Obedience

John now makes it plain that obedience to God's *commands* is not only related to love, as an evidence of faith, but it is actually the way in which we love God (3a). This is what gives love its moral fibre. We need to re-emphasize this, because we live in a generation where the sovereignty of emotions and feelings has come to mean that even the word 'love' has been emptied of its moral content.

We can so easily fall into the trap of opposing love to obedience. Because we love God, we truly want to please him, in our thoughts, words and actions. For us, it is no longer an external matter of moral duty in obeying a law so much as pleasing a dearly loved Father that lies at the heart of our Christian discipleship. And the glory of the new covenant is precisely the inner love for God which prompts obedience. But if we judge our love purely at the emotional level, without any regard for the moral obedience which God's law demands, we may well find ourselves excusing what is in fact disobedience, because we still feel warmly towards God. Just because we do not feel self-condemned does not mean that God is smiling on us. Indeed he cannot, if we are plainly transgressing his commandments, however much we may protest that we love him or claim a special relationship with him. The God of love never indulges the sin of disobedience. All sorts of moral disasters await those who try to separate clear-cut obedience to God's law from love for him.

Loving God is not expressing a liking for him, a preference in his direction. In 1982, I visited the 'city of brotherly love', Philadelphia, in the USA, for the first time. All over the city there were stickers bearing the message 'I love Philly', the word 'love' usually being replaced by a large red heart. I took it to mean 'I like it here', and I agreed! But I was especially keen to bring a sticker home with me because the same three words had a much greater depth of meaning for me. At home, I had a little daughter called Philippa, whose pet name in our family was and is Philly. For me, 'I love Philly' is not just an expression of pleasure or preference, it is a heart commitment which dictates many of my daily choices, and which may well involve me in a good deal of personal sacrifice, because I love my daughter. The two sorts of love are very different, but the second way is the only meaningful way to say 'I love God.' The heartbeat of God's love (*agapē*) for us is sacrifice (4:9–10), and there is no other sort of love with which we can respond to his initiative. To profess love for God but to fail to obey his commands is a nonsense. It shows that we are actually thinking that his commands are a bore, a chore, a heavy load (3b). And what does that say in turn about our attitude to God himself?

In fact, his commands are no more burdensome than wings are to a bird. They are the means by which we live in freedom and fulfilment, as God intended us to do. Did not the Lord Jesus himself promise us, 'My yoke is easy and my burden is light' (Matt. 11:30)? He was contrasting his commands with the heavy load of legalism with which the Pharisees burdened people's consciences. All they could do was cripple and paralyse those who submitted to the traditions of religious teachers. But Christ's commands are for our good. They are the 'maker's instructions' perfectly designed to meet his creatures' needs. 'In keeping them there is great reward' (Ps. 19:11), so he will give us strength to do what he has commanded and love will make our sense of burden light. It is sad that so many Christians today have relegated love to an emotional level alone and have caricatured any emphasis on the law of God as legalism. It is a false dichotomy that can actually unbalance the whole of our spiritual experience. We would hardly be commanded to love God and our neighbour if love were not a function of God's will. This does not mean that it is easy to fulfil God's commands, for we all retain an inbuilt bias away from God through our sinful human nature. But it is neither a solution nor an excuse to dismiss keeping the commandments as legalistic, and to lapse into the lawlessness of our secular culture. The prevailing fashion may be 'if it feels good, it is good', but Christians have other criteria by which to judge their behaviour. Christians keep God's commandments; not perfectly, of course, but characteristically.

This remains true of all of the marks of Christian reality which we have noted throughout John's letter. For example, Christians do not go on habitually practising sin (3:9). But they certainly sin (1:8), and God has provided forgiveness in the person of Jesus Christ, our advocate (2:1). Christians are not happy to remain in a state of sin. The new spiritual life implanted within them is constantly warring against the old sinful nature, and the more Christians abide in Christ and draw on the Saviour's limitless resources, the more they will experience increasing victory over sin. But the battle will never be finally won, in this life. The same is true of our desire to obey God's commands and of our love for him and for his children. We must not, however, make the mistake of distorting John's meaning by interpreting the letter as a series of contrasts between spiritual and carnal Christians. These verses, in common with the rest of the letter, are not saying that this is how Christians *ought* to behave, but how they *do*. The contrast throughout is between believers and unbelievers, those who have been truly born of God and those who have not, whatever they may profess. Only if we grasp that clearly shall we find the assurance which John's letter is written to give us.

c. Victory

Victory is the third and last characteristic evidence of true faith in a Christian's life and experience. Verse 4 begins with another deliberately inclusive statement: *everyone born of God overcomes the world.* The idea is not a new one in this letter. We saw as far back as 2:15–17 that this world as an organized system is implacably opposed to the things of God. It is under the control of the evil one (5:19). But the new birth removes us from that sphere of decay and death (2:17) and translates us into the kingdom of eternal life (3:14).

In Johannine terms, the clearest feature of the evil one and of the world system which he controls is the denial that Jesus is the Christ, the Son of God. Ever since the serpent's doom was pronounced in Genesis 3:14–15 – his head would be crushed by the woman's offspring – the enemy's tactics were to destroy the people of God and so prevent the coming of the deliverer. And since Christ has come, all the devil's efforts have been directed towards denying his deity and the historicity of his humanity and life. But once a man or woman comes to believe that Jesus is Christ, the Son of God, the enemy's hold on that person is broken for ever. It is this key which opens the prison-house and sets us free to be our true, redeemed selves, in Christ. We should not be surprised that the world does all it can to deny that. When the media give far more attention and time to those who deny Christ than to those who believe, that is simply the world being true to its presuppositions. There is only one way to overcome the world, and that is our faith *that Jesus is the Son of God* (4b–5).

There is an important check to remember here, however; John's emphasis is on the power of the victory rather than on the persons who share it. This seems to be why the original in verse 4a has 'everything' (neuter) *born of God* rather than 'everyone', which would have been masculine, as in verse 1 and later in verse 18. The personal ingredient is emphasized at the end of verse 4. It is *our* faith and *we* have to believe the message. But our believing is not the means by which victory over the world is achieved. Rather, it is the new birth from God which conquers. Indeed, the aorist tense in verse 4b (*has overcome*) indicates a victory which has been achieved once and for all. Our minds go back to the great events of the crucifixion and resurrection of the Lord Jesus where the victory was accomplished. This is the object of our faith – Jesus, the Son of God, and his eternal work of salvation – and in this faith alone we can and do conquer. The victory is already ours in Christ. All that he has done for his people is the substance of our faith. But the victory has to be appropriated in our daily experience, and that occurs as we exercise our faith.

So verse 5 moves us into the present tense and the potential daily experience of Christ's victory in our own discipleship, available to us all as Christian believers. Everything depends upon our union with Christ, by faith, through which the divine resources are made available to all who trust him so that we too may be victorious in our battle with the world, the flesh and the devil. We cannot share God's victory if we do not believe in his Son. For Jesus is the only source of the divine power which is strong enough to overcome our enemies. That has to be believed in practice and in action, or there will be no power. But wherever that faith is central and active, there is victory. Again we have to stress that this is not to say that the conflict is over, but that the *outcome* is settled, and that nothing in this world or beyond can overcome the believer who is rooted in Christ (see Rom. 8:37–39). After all, this was what Jesus himself promised. 'In this world you will have trouble,' he told his disciples on the last night he was with them. 'But take heart! I have overcome the world' (John 16:33). And all those who are united to him, in this faith, have also overcome.

Our practical problem so often is to believe these things to be true. It is in this area of faith that we are most conscious of our weakness. We look around at the frightful power of evil in the world, with its apparently inexorable onward march that nothing can stop. We feel the force of temptation in our own lives and find ourselves falling into sin. We identify only too easily with Paul's desperate cry in Romans 7:24, 'What a wretched man I am! Who will rescue me from this body that is subject to death?' But we need equally to share his conviction in the next verse: 'Thanks be to God . . . through Jesus Christ our Lord!' It is only as we firmly grasp who Jesus really is and what power he has that all the apparent superiority of the hostile forces is put into its true perspective. Only then do we realize that this world and its desires are passing away (2:17) and that what looks so strong and immovable is actually decaying and doomed to destruction. And this faith is not escapism; on the contrary, it is the only ultimate realism. For, as Howard Marshall reminds us, 'It rests foursquare on the fact that Jesus Christ has defeated death, and anybody who can defeat death can defeat anything.'[3]

So God calls us to a life of faith, demonstrated by love for him and for one another, by obedience to his commands and by victory over the world. As we exercise that faith, we find that it works. God keeps his promises and fulfils his Word. As we believe that when God says 'Do this', or 'Not that', he knows what is best for us, we do what he says, trust him with the consequences and prove him to be true. When we are living that way, the world cannot trap or deceive us. This sort of faith is the only way to victory. When we think carefully about them, at root all our defeats are failures of faith; failures to trust or to obey, or both. The potential, God's dynamic, is always on supply. What faith does is to connect my situation

---

[3] Marshall, p. 229.

to God's resources, rather like plugging my electrical machinery into the power circuit. Only then will the light of God's truth overcome the darkness of this world's lies, and the warmth of God's love expel the coldness of this world's self-centredness.

Such faith is not irrational, though it may transcend our human reasoning process. It is the nature of faith to act on evidence, and it is usually at its strongest when it knows why, as well as what, it believes. Indeed, so-called 'blind' faith can actually be very harmful. That is why the Bible's stress is always on the content of truth, the object of our faith.

I remember driving down a motorway in a very heavy snowstorm. It was not long before all the lane markings were completely obliterated. Then it began to get dark. Speed-restriction lights were flashing and conditions were very dangerous. There were some drivers (a few!) who responded to all this 'evidence', took in the warnings and observed the speed limits. But many, probably the majority, ploughed on regardless with hardly any concessions to the conditions, presumably in the blind faith that accidents are what happen to other people. That is not the sort of 'faith' (or credulity) John is looking for. Those who responded to the evidence on the motorway were much more likely to 'overcome', and survive, than those who ignored it or chose to hope against hope. Christians are called to be realists, living in a world structured by God, where causes do produce effects, and where there are both material and spiritual laws. If so much depends upon believing the truth, we must make sure that the evidence is firm and reliable.

1 John 5:6–12

17. Evidence – the key to faith

The faith that overcomes the world is the very specific belief 'that Jesus is the Son of God' (5:5). This was precisely what Cerinthus and the other false teachers were denying when they insisted that Jesus was the natural son of Joseph and Mary. But, as John has shown us throughout the letter, to dispense with the deity of Jesus is to dispense with the only way by which we human beings can come into any fellowship with the living God (3:23–24; 1:6). The false teaching did not stop there, however. It went on to claim that the 'aeon' (divine emanation), Christ, was joined to Jesus, the natural son of Joseph, at his baptism in order to equip him for his ministry – only to leave him again at his passion to die as nothing more than an ordinary man. For them Jesus was a great man, a fine teacher and a wonderful example. He might even prove to be an intermediary (one among many) between God and humanity. But he was not the eternal Son of God, the second person of the holy Trinity, the Word made flesh. Although the route by which they reach such a conclusion may be different, that is exactly what millions of people in the Western world today would give as their answer to the question, 'Who was Jesus?' These verses are designed by John to refute such erroneous opinions.

He begins with the robust assertion *This* [Jesus, the Son of God; verse 5] *is the one who came.* The Greek form of the words *the one who came* (an aorist participle) indicates the once-for-all, historical fact of his coming into the world, sent by the Father (4:9–10). So once more John stresses the identity of the historical person of Jesus of Nazareth, a real man who really lived in time and space, with the eternal Son of God. Westcott underlines this by claiming that this term *the one who came* is used 'with a clear reference to the technical sense of "he that cometh" (*ho erchomenos*)'.[1] This would relate what John is saying about Jesus to the messianic title 'he who comes', taken up and ascribed to Jesus by the Palm Sunday crowds at his entry into Jerusalem (Matt. 21:9 and John 12:13). Or again, the title was used by John the Baptist as he pointed his own followers to Jesus, witnessing to the fact that Jesus was the one whose coming had been promised long before (John 1:15, 27). The same title was again used by John the Baptist when, disillusioned and discouraged, he sent two of his disciples to the Lord to ask, 'Are you *the one who is to come*, or should we expect someone else?' (Luke 7:19; emphasis added). Westcott concludes that 'the one who came' 'is equivalent to He that fulfilled the promises to the fathers, as the Saviour sent from God'.[2] At all events, John is asserting the historicity of the incarnation as the foundation stone of his defence of Christ's deity.

He now proceeds to assemble his evidence.

1. The three witnesses (5:6–9)

Jesus *came by water and blood* (6b). The preposition *by* is literally 'by means of' or 'through', and it is probably best for us to keep in mind that water and blood are to be seen as the means by which Jesus came into the world to accomplish his mission of salvation. From Augustine onwards, a long line of commentators has interpreted this to mean the water and blood which flowed from the side of Christ when pierced by the spear as he hung on the cross (see John 19:34–35). In that context, John emphatically underlines his eyewitness 'testimony' to this real death of a real man. The link with *testimony* in these verses, and the claim that only in these two passages are blood and water brought together, have been used to support this as the primary reference; though Plummer refutes the latter point with eight other references.[3] It seems very unlikely that John would build such a major argument on such a comparatively small historical detail, even if he was an eyewitness. Others have drawn attention to the water of baptism and the blood (wine) of the Eucharist, and have seen here a symbolic foreshadowing of the two great sacraments of the church. These

---

[1] Westcott, p. 181.

[2] Ibid.

[3] Five in Exod. 7:17–25; also Lev. 14:52; Matt. 27:24; Heb. 9:19; Plummer, p. 113.

things may well be true, but they do not sufficiently account for John's meaning in its own context.

In what sense did Jesus 'come' *by water*? This cannot be a reference simply to his physical birth, as a human being, since that matter was not under dispute. Much more likely and pertinent is that the beginning of the ministry of Jesus, when his 'coming' began to be widely revealed, was marked by water in his baptism in the River Jordan (see Mark 1:9–11). Not only was this the public beginning of his ministry, it was also a divine witness to his identity. The Spirit descended upon him, like a dove, and the voice of God was heard affirming that this was his beloved Son with whom he was well pleased. It was a coming by water to take up the work which the Father had entrusted to him.

Although they would have put a different construction upon the event, seeing it as the moment at which the human Jesus received the divine Spirit as a temporary endowment, the false teachers would have had no difficulty in affirming that the Christ had come in, or by, water. What John is at pains to stress is that *he did not come by water only, but by water and blood* (6). He means that the one who came, whom Christians confess to be the Son of God, was as fully and thoroughly the eternal Son, the Christ, at his death as he was at his baptism or his birth. The Jesus who died on the cross was not just a man from whom the divine Spirit had been withdrawn; he was nothing less than God. He *came by . . . blood*. The purpose of his coming, explained at his baptism, was fulfilled only in his sacrificial death. The same Son of God became the atoning sacrifice for our sins, and it is faith in him alone and in his completed work that brings eternal life, love for God and for his children, and victory over the world.

There is a third 'witness' mentioned in verse 6. *It is the Spirit who testifies, because the Spirit is the truth*. Here John goes behind his own role and that of his fellow apostles as those who have seen and therefore testify (1:2; 4:14), to reveal the ultimate authority and undergirding of what they declare, in the Spirit who is the truth. We may reject Augustine's view that the 'spirit' referred to is the human spirit of Jesus committed to his Father in death – a view over-conditioned by Augustine's linking of the water and blood exclusively to the events of Calvary. It is unlikely that John would call the human spirit of Jesus *the truth*. If, in common with the majority of interpreters, we accept this to be a reference to the Holy Spirit, we make much more biblical sense of it.

To pursue John's metaphor of the witness box in a court of law, when the Holy Spirit is called to testify he does not need to declare, 'I swear by almighty God that I will tell the truth.' He is God. All our concepts of truth derive from him, as the practice of our law courts daily affirms. So the Spirit himself bears witness because he *is* the truth. There is no truth apart from God, for truth is grounded in God's character alone. Truth is not the majority view in the opinion poll. It is not feeling good about something. It is not an emotional encounter. All truth is God's truth, because only he is the ultimate reality.

It is the function of the Spirit, then, to testify to the truth, as it is in Jesus. This was what the Lord Jesus himself had promised his disciples.

When the Advocate comes, whom I will send to you from the Father – the Spirit of truth who goes out from the Father – he will testify about me. And you also must testify, for you have been with me from the beginning.
(John 15:26–27)

The apostles were the human channels through which the truth was relayed. The Spirit was their guarantor and enabler. And how does the Spirit testify today but through the channels he commissioned and used at the beginning, through the apostolic testimony, the New Testament? Again, this is a direct fulfilment of the promise of Jesus, recorded by John in his Gospel: 'when he, the Spirit of truth, comes, he will guide you into all truth. He will not speak on his own; he will speak only what he hears, and he will tell you what is yet to come' (John 16:13).

So the Spirit bears witness through the Scriptures, God's Word of truth, by which human minds are instructed and human wills are changed, as he brings Christ's obedient followers increasingly into likeness to their Lord. The Spirit of God still takes the Word of God and produces children of God. Or, in the words of the Westminster Confession, 'our full persuasion and assurance of the infallible truth [of the Bible] is from the work of the Holy Spirit, bearing witness by and with the Word in our hearts'.[4] This explains how the lives of three thousand people were transformed on the day of Pentecost. It was not that they had discovered new evidence concerning the resurrection or the deity of Christ. That objective

---

[4] Westminster Confession 1.4, quoted by Clark, p. 155.

evidence had been there ever since Easter morning. It was the activity of the Spirit 'testifying' to the truth and to the person of Christ that brought a multitude to faith, as they repented, found forgiveness and were baptized (Acts 2:36–41). It is still the same today.

So the three witnesses are assembled (7) and are found to be in complete agreement (8). This is an important ingredient in the confidence we can have in their veracity. Verse 7 actually begins with 'Because', translated as *For* in the NIV. It is because there are three witnesses, so united, that we can have certainty, since in any court of law this would provide the strongest evidence of truth. In Jewish law it was necessary to have two or three witnesses for a case to be carried (Deut. 17:6; 19:15). It was a principle recognized by Jesus (John 5:31–37) who adduced John the Baptist, the work that he was doing and the Father who sent him as authentication of his witness and claims. Even God himself, wanting 'to make the unchanging nature of his purpose very clear to the heirs of what was promised', confirmed his promise with an oath – 'two unchangeable things in which it is impossible for God to lie' (Heb. 6:17–18). Here, the three witnesses all agree that Jesus is the Son of God, just as John testified at his baptism (John 1:34) and the centurion testified at his death (Matt. 27:54). So, whenever that same Spirit brings the truth to light in our lives today, we are brought to confess Jesus as Saviour, Lord and God. Yet human witness is of little significance in comparison with God's own witness to his own truth.

Readers of modern translations will realize that the extraordinary shortness of verse 7 is due to an omission from the text of several lines, found in the Textus Receptus and translated in the Authorized Version of 1611. The NIV footnote addition would give the following reading:

For there are three that testify in heaven: the Father, the Word and the Holy Spirit, and these three are one. And there are three that testify on earth: the Spirit, the water and the blood; and the three are in agreement.
(7–8)

They are completely ignored by the RSV and NEB since they do not occur in any of the Greek manuscripts of 1 John before the fourteenth century, and then in only six, all of them late and so of very little value. The words came from a fifth-century Old Latin version and were incorporated into the

Vulgate about AD 800, where they remained. F. F. Bruce, in a lucid discussion of the matter, tells how Erasmus was attacked for omitting the 'three heavenly witnesses' in his first printed edition of the Greek New Testament (1516). He replied that he would include them only if a Greek manuscript could be produced in which they were contained. Such a manuscript was eventually produced, written about 1520! Erasmus duly kept his word, although he realized that this was no evidence at all, and incorporated the extra text in his third edition (1522). Luther translated this into German and Tyndale into English. Other printed editions of the Greek New Testament also included it, and by this route it was incorporated into the Textus Receptus and the Authorized Version of 1611.[5] Perhaps the strongest evidence against the reading is that it is not quoted by any of the early Church Fathers, who, in their battles with the heretics, would only too gladly have seized on the text as a clear biblical testimony to the Trinity, had it existed.[6]

This brings us to verse 9, where John reminds us that *we accept human testimony, but God's testimony is greater*. In what sense? We realize, of course, that God is infinitely greater in his eternal nature and power than finite, mortal human beings. But John is wanting to convey both the greater trustworthiness of God's testimony because of its origin, and also its greater importance and value because of its content. *It is the testimony of God, which he has given about his Son* (9). Probably the locus of that testimony to which John wants to direct our attention is the baptism of Jesus. There the Father's voice and the Spirit's descent unite the Trinity in powerful witness that Jesus is the Son of God. That is the content of the Christian gospel. It is stated and authenticated by God himself and confirmed by his three witnesses. If we would accept human testimony under such circumstances (and we most certainly would), how can we refuse to accept the divine?

2. The fourth dimension (5:10–12)

I suppose we could call this further witness the personal, or subjective, dimension of faith. Certainly it is internal. Verse 10 begins, literally, 'He who is believing in the Son of God has the testimony in himself' (see RSV).

---

[5] Bruce, pp. 129–130.
[6] Marshall, p. 236.

But clearly there are dangers here, not least in the over-subjectivism or mysticism into which both liberal and conservative Christians may fall. Many contemporary theologians, following Bultmann and Brunner, would want to stress that the only authentication needed for faith is the inner, personal witness, irrespective of history or the Bible. It is the existential encounter of the individual with the Christ of faith which validates belief in the resurrection, however that may be defined. From a totally different perspective, evangelical Christians will readily affirm that Christ living within them is the guarantee of the reality of their faith and of his resurrection. 'I know that Jesus is alive,' they assert, 'because I spoke to him this morning.' The question that must be asked is, 'How do you know you are not deluding yourself?' All sorts of people do delude themselves in both their emotions and their experiences.

What John is affirming is that this testimony is in the Christian because he or she is believing in the Son of God. The Greek present participle (*ho pisteuōn*, the one who believes) indicates a permanent and continuous action. The preposition *eis* (in), which follows, shows that John means much more than simply believing what Christ says, in the sense of understanding or even accepting it. To believe 'in' or 'on' Christ is to commit oneself to him as fully as one knows in faithful reliance on him. This is, of course, John's favourite description of saving faith in his Gospel, where he uses *pisteuō eis* on over forty occasions. It is as we meet the historical Jesus, through the apostolic testimony and the work of the Spirit, that the objective realities of all that he accomplished for us in his death and resurrection become internalized in our experience now. The new birth takes place and following it there develops the growing inner conviction that these things are true and they are true in and for us as individuals.

We must be careful to preserve John's strong emphasis on believing, intensified by the negative correlative in the second part of verse 10. For it is not our subjective experience of Christ that saves us, but our believing in him, which is then confirmed and deepened by the inner witness of the Spirit. This agrees with Paul's teaching in Romans 8:16, 'The Spirit himself testifies with our spirit that we are God's children', and Galatians 4:6, 'Because you are his sons, God sent the Spirit of his Son into our hearts, the Spirit who calls out *"Abba*, Father."'

It is a major theme of biblical theology that God wants his people to be assured of their relationship with him as reconciled, forgiven sinners. The only alternative is actually to make God out to be a liar (10b). That is how clearly the Bible draws the line between faith in Jesus and unbelief. This is not surprising when we consider how strong is the evidence for faith that has been presented to us. There is an element of unwillingness to believe, seen in the rejection of the witness which God has given and is still giving, through the activity of his Spirit, concerning his Son. There is ample evidence for faith, but our problem is not ignorance so much as rebellion; not that we *cannot* believe but rather that we *will* not. (See Paul's argument in Romans 1:18–25.) Biblical theology was turned into prayer as Charles Wesley grasped this great reality and built upon it, asking for the Holy Spirit to move in convicting and converting power:

Spirit of faith, come down,
    Reveal the things of God;
And make to us the Godhead known,
    And witness with the blood.
'Tis thine the blood to apply
    And give us eyes to see;
Who did for every sinner die
    Hath surely died for me.

Inspire the living faith,
    Which whosoe'er receives,
The witness in himself he hath,
    And consciously believes;
That faith that conquers all,
    And doth the mountain move,
And saves whoe'er on Jesus call
    And perfects them in love.[7]

Verses 11 and 12 must stand as among the most magnificent in the whole of the New Testament. The consequences of believing God's truth or denying it could hardly be more important or far-reaching. John is not merely concerned about academic disagreements over theological niceties. Eternal destinies are at stake. *Eternal life* (*zōē aiōnios*) means literally the life of eternity, the life of the world to come. Yet this is

---

[7] 'Spirit of Faith, Come Down', by Charles Wesley (1707–88).

something which God has already given to those who believe in Jesus. It is the present possession of every Christian believer.

This is not difficult to understand when we remember that one of the favourite pictures of the life and ministry of Jesus in the Synoptic Gospels is that of the breaking through of the kingdom of the heavens (or of God) into the space–time context of this world. In Jesus, the invisible God has revealed himself in terms that can be understood anywhere, any time – a perfect human life. In Jesus, the powers of the unseen world, the age to come, are being revealed as he demonstrates his sovereignty over all the hostile forces ranged against humanity – sin, disease, demons, and even death itself. Supremely, the life of eternity is life that has overcome the grave, and that life can be found in Christ alone who triumphed over death by his glorious resurrection. *This life is in his Son.*

Not surprisingly, this is a theme developed very extensively in John's Gospel, which underlines that only in Jesus can such life be known and experienced. So to the unbelieving Jews who were trying to kill him because 'he was even calling God his own Father, making himself equal with God' (John 5:18), Jesus unambiguously declared, 'Just as the Father raises the dead and gives them life, even so the Son gives life to whom he is pleased to give it' (John 5:21). And again, 'As the Father has life in himself, so he has granted the Son also to have life in himself' (John 5:26). He concludes, 'Yet you refuse to come to me to have life' (John 5:40). Later, to the crowds still marvelling at the feeding of the five thousand, Jesus declares himself to be the bread of life, for which they are craving, and continues, 'For my Father's will is that everyone who looks to the Son and believes in him shall have eternal life, and I will raise them up at the last day' (John 6:40). Speaking of his sheep, as the Good Shepherd Jesus promises, 'I give them eternal life, and they shall never perish; no one will snatch them out of my hand' (John 10:28). Then, in the very face of death itself, with Lazarus four days in the tomb, he declares to Martha, 'I am the resurrection and the life. The one who believes in me will live, even though they die; and whoever lives by believing in me will never die' (John 11:25–26). With this dominant theme running through John's Gospel, we are not surprised to find that it recurs in the most intimate chapter of all, chapter 17. Here the Son is reviewing in prayer all that has happened in his ministry before committing himself, his disciples and the future church to the Father. The work he is now about to complete is seen in terms of eternal life:

For you granted him authority over all people that he might give eternal life to all those you have given him. Now this is eternal life: that they know you, the only true God, and Jesus Christ, whom you have sent. (John 17:2–3)

What John is saying in his letter is not a new claim. It runs throughout his Gospel account of Jesus' ministry. *This life is in his Son* and nowhere else. But it is experienced here, or it will not be experienced in the world beyond (12). Those who do not believe that Jesus is the Son cannot have him as their Saviour, neither can they have the eternal life only he can give. John's focus is undoubtedly on the false teachers who demonstrated that they did not have the Son by denying his incarnation and deity (4:2). As such, they stood under sentence of death. What could be simpler, or more profound?

The picture which Scripture itself uses to illuminate our understanding of this life-giving relationship between Christ and his church is the human covenant of marriage (see, for example, Eph. 5:22–33). By this contract of two wills, one new unit ('one flesh', Gen. 2:24) is formed. Marriage begins with a specific action in time, which has an effect on the whole of the future. There is a definite commitment, however long or whirlwind the courtship may have been, which marks a new way of life. When a person is asked, 'Are you married?', the answer may be 'Yes' or 'No', but can hardly be 'I'm not sure'! So it is with the covenant of the new birth, by which we have eternal life. On one side, Christians recognize Christ's authority and submit their wills to him. On the other side, the Lord Jesus lovingly accepts sinners, calling them as his own and binding himself to his people by covenant promises that can never be broken. It is the quality of commitment affirmed by a bride and groom to each other as they give and receive rings in their marriage service, saying, 'All that I am I give to you, and all that I have I share with you.'[8] The Lord will never break his covenant vows. He draws us to trust him before we ever confess that faith in him. As he brings us into this living union with himself, through faith, we receive here and now the life of the eternal. For if the Son has this life in himself, then whoever has the Son has life. And those who have him know him to be the Son of God. Upon our relationship with him depends the future destiny of every one of us.

---

[8] The Marriage Service, paragraphs 14 and 15 (*Alternative Service Book*).

1 John 5:13–21

18. You can be sure

When I was an undergraduate, reading English, the entire university faculty was riven with different factions warring against each other, based on different theories about, or approaches to, the business of literary criticism. As with some of the divisions between denominational groupings within the church, one felt that the feuding parties often owed more in blind loyalty to their charismatic leaders than to their scholarship or academic objectivity. My own director of studies was at the epi-centre of these controversies, and had the strongest views on those members of the faculty who 'knew' about literature (and who agreed with his approach) and those who did not. Declaiming one day against a rival theorist, he reached the peak of his dismissive anger with the statement, 'He doesn't know, you know, and what is more he doesn't know he doesn't know!'

That is certainly what the false teachers were saying about the apostle John, with their argument that true *gnōsis* (knowledge) could be acquired only through their own esoteric insights. This was the controversy which beset the church. Were those who stood in the orthodox tradition of apos-tolic testimony and faith, as expounded in this letter, deluded? Or were they right to believe as they did? Clearly the claim that there was higher knowledge, and with it perhaps a more tangible subjective certainty, was having an erosive effect on the straightforward orthodoxy of many believers. No doubt this would be caricatured as 'simple' and 'unsophisti-cated'. When an attractive alternative is on offer, purporting to go deeper or take its adherents further into spiritual reality, the keenest Christians are going to be the most vulnerable.

The issues at stake are not speculative or academic. The question at issue is where *eternal life* is to be found and experienced. We are to read verse 13, therefore, not simply as a concluding statement about the purpose of the letter, but as the climactic assertion to which the preceding chapters have been relentlessly moving. *These things* must surely refer to the whole letter rather than simply to the immediately preceding sentences. When John began his letter, he expressed his purpose in writing, 'to make our joy complete' (1:4). Now he shows us what the content of that joy is. It comes in seeing his 'dear children' continuing in the faith, believing in the name of the Son of God and rejoicing in the certainty of eternal life. Joy, for the apostle, for his 'children', and for Christians in every generation, is found in the conscious experience of fellowship with God the Father, through Jesus the Son, within the community of his family, the church.

In John's two shorter letters we shall find the same note being struck. 'It has given me great joy to find some of your children walking in the truth' (2 John 4). Or again, 'I have no greater joy than to hear that my children are walking in the truth' (3 John 4). This was why the great apostle had written his letter. In the Gospel (John 20:31) he tells us that he wrote 'that you may believe that Jesus is the Messiah, the Son of God, and that by believing you may have life in his name'. Now he has written *so that you may know that you have eternal life*. It is the joy of assurance, leading to the discipline of faithful perseverance in the truth, that is his heart's desire for his readers.

It is because eternal life is 'knowing God' (John 17:3) that Christians can have absolute confidence of their assurance. *Eternal life* is a personal-encounter knowledge of God, leading on to a lifetime of fellowship with him, which cannot be counterfeited. But again John stresses that it is only by affirming the incarnation of the Son of God that one may be said truly to believe in who Jesus is. In common with biblical usage generally, 'believing in the name of the Son of God' here means believing in his nature as the Son of God. Bible names are not mere labels, without content, as our names usually are today, at least in the Western world. The name in Scripture stands for the nature or character of a person. So no claim to have eternal life can stand if the claimant is denying the essential deity of Christ, in whom alone eternal life can be experienced. Not only does John want his readers to have an incontrovertible personal encounter with God in Christ; he also wants their belief to be solidly grounded, intellectually and theologically, as they clearly understand why eternal life can be found nowhere else, and what the non-negotiable ingredients of that saving faith really are. Only that sort of certainty would be able to undergird and strengthen them when the gnostic false teachers came with their persuasive arguments and impressive rhetoric, claiming that they alone were 'in the know'. But although this is the primary reference of this marvellous statement, in great gratitude to God we can agree with F. F. Bruce that 'because of its abiding validity it has remained a classic and effective text conveying the assurance of eternal life in all generations to those who believe in the name of the Son of God'.[1]

So strong are the ringing tones of this confident assertion that some modern commentators have suggested that verse 13 marks the end of the letter, the remaining verses being an addendum by John or someone else. The same kind of comments are often made about chapter 21 of John's Gospel. But there are no extant manuscripts from which verses 14–21 are missing; their vocabulary and structure are consistent with John's; and they are quoted by Clement of Alexandria and Tertullian, who mention John by name as their author. We do not, therefore, need to spend more time with these conjectures. Rather, as we turn to the remaining verses, we shall see how their themes reiterate interests we have already seen in the letter, and how they highlight for us four ways in which these God-given certainties can be deepened as we work out our faith in practice.

1. A new assurance in prayer (5:14–17)

The first characteristic of our knowing God, that relationship which is eternal life, is *confidence* in our approach to him (14a). This will naturally be expressed in prayer, where the mark of Christian reality is *parrēsia*, 'boldness', or perhaps better, 'freedom of speech'. Our conversation with God is to be uninhibited, open and relaxed, yet not without reverence and submission. Its manner reflects the fact that we are children of a loving heavenly Father.

John is not the only New Testament writer to highlight this quality. In Hebrews 4:16 we read that, because Jesus is our high priest, who knows our temptations and understands our weaknesses, we can 'approach God's throne of grace with confidence [*parrēsia*], so that we may receive mercy and find grace to help us in our time of need'. And John has already used

---

[1] Bruce, p. 123.

the term three times to teach us that as Christians we can be confident at the return of Jesus, if we continue in him (2:28). This is because on the judgment day, the process of becoming like Jesus in this world will be completed (4:17). Moreover, in 3:21, John has related this confidence to prayer; we can pray confidently because God in his sovereignty knows us and forgives us. The teaching of Jesus on the night of his betrayal, recorded by John in chapters 14–16 of his Gospel, is full of similar encouragements. These obviously became formative in John's own prayer life and teaching on prayer. Had not the Master promised, 'You may ask me for anything in my name, and I will do it' (John 14:14)? Such confidence both results from 'believing in the name of the Son of God' and proves the reality of that life-giving faith.

Verse 14 does, however, introduce a limitation on such confident praying; or, more accurately, it underlines and explains the restriction that the Lord Jesus himself placed on asking. It must be *according to his will* if he is to hear us. Within that proviso, we may *ask anything*. Our praying is never on a surer foundation than when it is grounded in Scripture, for here God's will is revealed. As we pray Bible prayers, we know that God will hear and answer.

Of course, we still have to make sure that, at our human end, we are not vitiating our prayers by unbelief or disobedience. 'If I had cherished sin in my heart, the Lord would not have listened' (Ps. 66:18). It is hypocritical nonsense to hold on to some cherished sin in our lives and at the same time come to God in prayer, to ask him for some gracious good gift. But if we have first found his cleansing and forgiveness (1:9), we can ask with boldness. God's will is 'good, pleasing and perfect' (Rom. 12:2), so when a request is refused it is not due to any reluctance or unwillingness in God, unless it be the unwillingness to give to a dearly loved child something that the heavenly Father, in his perfect wisdom, knows would not be in that child's best interests.

For prayer is not an attempt to get God to see things my way and to extract from him what I have decided I need or want. Prayer is submitting my will to his. To paraphrase the Lord's Prayer, it is saying, 'Your will be done in me, your bit of earth, as it is in Christ, who is my heaven!' It is opening the door of my need to the Lord Jesus. And this means that prayer is God's means by which my submission to Christ's lordship can be developed. The less I pray, the more self-willed I become. But the corollary is wonderfully true. 'Not my will, but yours' – that is the essence of assured prayer, the secret of prevailing prayer. What confidence we can have! This should be a great stimulus in our personal lives to find out God's will, to build on the commands and promises of his Word in our prayers, to talk every situation through with him, and to submit all our thinking, planning and deciding to God. Answers to prayer do not depend on a right diagnosis or analysis of the problem by us as we pray, but on a childlike submission to the Father, knowing that he will give what is best *according to his will.* If he were to answer on any other basis, which of us would ever dare to pray again? We do not have that sort of wisdom.

A further confidence in verse 15 is that we can know that, with God, to hear is to answer. This is the force of the present tense *we have what we asked.* There is no 'pending' tray with God. Though from our perspective the outworking of the answer may not be seen until sometime in the future, our requests are granted at once. The trust that opens up our needs to God is not disappointed.

There is a graphic Old Testament illustration in the book of Daniel. At the beginning of chapter 10, Daniel receives a revelation from God concerning a great war. He begins a period of fasting and mourning to give himself to prayer, and after three weeks an angelic messenger appears to him in a vision. The description is so similar to that of the glorified Lord in Revelation 1:13–16 (and the devastating effect on Daniel as great as that on John) that many believe this to be an appearance of Christ. But the significant factor is that the messenger says,

> Do not be afraid, Daniel. Since the first day that you set your mind to gain understanding and to humble yourself before your God, your words were heard, and I have come in response to them. But the prince of the Persian kingdom resisted me twenty-one days.
> (Dan. 10:12–13)

The answer to Daniel's prayer was immediate; but his experience of it was not. The reason given was the cosmic spiritual warfare that was being waged, and in which Daniel was engaged through his praying. When we take the weapon of prayer (Eph. 6:18), we do become involved in the struggle 'not against flesh and blood, but against the rulers, against the authorities, against the powers of this dark world and against the spiritual forces of evil in the heavenly realms' (Eph. 6:12). This is one explanation why we may not seem to have what we have asked for, and why we can speak of answers to prayer being delayed. But it is also a great encouragement to go on praying in confidence, knowing that our praying can play its part in the spiritual battle.

Now we must turn to verses 16–17, which have proved to be so difficult to interpret down through the centuries. There are several related issues here, the central one being what John means by *a sin that does not lead to death* and *a sin that leads to death* (16). In the former case, Christians are exhorted to *pray* for a *brother or sister* whom they see sinning; in the latter, they are not. What is the distinction between the two? Are there distinguishing features for which we should look?

The traditional Roman Catholic view is that there are two categories of sin: 'venial' (pardonable), and 'mortal' (sin that leads to death). The seven deadly sins are literally so, though the sacrament of penance, prescribed by the Church through the priest, is designed to be a work of penitence by which satisfaction for sin can be made. The text, however, offers no support for such a division of sins, much less for a list of mortal sins. In the Bible's view every sin is mortal, since every sin pays the wage of eternal death (Rom. 6:23). Further, the New Testament offers no support for the belief that any human work can justify the guilty sinner. Indeed, this very letter of John reminds us that only the sacrifice of the Son of God can atone for sin by turning away God's wrath (e.g. 2:2; 4:10).

Others have suggested that the only way *sin that leads to death* could be identified is by its consequences in a literal physical sense. The fate of Ananias and Sapphira (Acts 5:1–11), and the references in 1 Corinthians to an immoral man being handed over to Satan 'for the destruction of the flesh' (1 Cor. 5:5) and to some who have 'fallen asleep' (1 Cor. 11:30) because of their abuse of the Lord's Supper, are all quoted in support of this view. If this interpretation is correct, John is discouraging prayer for such people since it would mean praying for the dead.[2] While this is clearly possible, we need to remember that in context the contrast is with 'eternal life', so that spiritual, rather than physical, death is the most natural reading of the text.

Others have identified the *sin that leads to death* with the 'blasphemy against the Spirit', often referred to as the unforgivable sin (see Matt. 12:31–32). The connection depends on the distinction that is drawn between this and all other sins, in that this sin, being unpardonable, must 'lead to death'. But it is worth noting that John says nothing about the Holy Spirit in this context, though that is precisely the sin's distinguishing

---

2 Bruce, pp. 124–125.

mark in the Gospels. Others suggest that John's reference is to the Old Testament concept of sinning 'defiantly' (Num. 15:30–31), among them S. Greijdanus who asserts that it is 'a fully conscious, deliberate sinning for the sake of sinning, in order to deny the Lord'.[3] If this interpretation is adopted, much will depend on the content given to the unpardonable sin. 'Whoever blasphemes against the Holy Spirit will never be forgiven; they are guilty of an eternal sin' (Mark 3:29).

Many sensitive Christians have suffered great anguish, and still do, imagining some particular sin of theirs to be unforgivable, or that in a rash moment they might commit the unpardonable sin. Indeed, because this sin has been surrounded by so much 'mystery', it has been the object of so much fear. That cannot be helpful, either to our understanding or to our spiritual health. Perhaps the most mysterious element is that such a sin can exist at all, given that we have such a gracious God who loves to pardon and to reconcile. Christian ministers may rightly try to counsel distressed Christians by pointing out that any real dread is a sure indication that they are not guilty of this sin.

One certainty must be that those who are most guilty are least concerned about their state. For it is not the magnitude of the sin that prevents its pardon, as though there existed this one sin for which Christ's sacrifice was insufficient. Rather, it is the attitude and disposition of the sinner that excludes the possibility of forgiveness. This was Augustine's insight when he defined the blasphemy against the Spirit as *impoenitentia finales*, final impenitence.

> The sin against the Spirit is not an acting against one's better conscience or a persecuting of the Church of Christ, but an apostatizing from Christ and his Kingdom even though one already has the knowledge of Christ through the Spirit. Therefore it is a falling away in a very conscious rebellion against the Kingdom of God's grace.[4]

While taking issue with Augustine's definition, Calvin

> defined this sin as a resistance in one's heart against the truth of God, even though one is touched with the glory of that truth and cannot

---

[3] Quoted in G. C. Berkouwer, *Sin* (Eerdmans, 1971), p. 333 n. 28.

[4] Berkouwer, op. cit., p. 342.

plead ignorance. Therefore this sin is seen as a bitter and hard-hearted resistance.[5]

All of these suggestions have some biblical warrant and are undoubtedly true in themselves, but are they what John was primarily concerned about? If his major emphasis as the letter concludes is that only those who believe that Jesus is the Son of God have eternal life (5, 13), then the sin that leads to death, the sin that excludes the sinner from the life of God, must surely be the denial of that saving truth. If this is right, then the sin that leads to death does so because, by its very nature, it rejects the only means by which sin may be forgiven – the atoning death of the incarnate Son of God. This underlines the important truth that it is not that this sin is *unpardonable*, but that it *remains unpardoned*. We need to preserve this distinction because so much of the rest of the letter has carefully established it. Purification from *every* sin has already been assured through 'the blood of Jesus' (1:7), so Christians are those whose sins (all of them) have been forgiven (2:12). Yet no believer in Christ can reckon him- or herself sinless, or imagine that he or she can dispense with a continuing forgiveness (1:8), so we need constantly to confess our sins and to call upon Christ for pardon and purification from *all* unrighteousness (1:9).

The sin that leads to death is unforgiven and remains unforgiven because it refuses to appropriate the gracious means of pardon which God has provided.

> Death is its natural, but not its absolutely inevitable consequence.
> It is possible to close the heart against the influences of God's Spirit
> so obstinately and persistently that repentance becomes a moral
> impossibility. Just as the body may starve itself to such an extent as
> to make the digestion, or even the reception, of food impossible; so the
> soul may go on refusing offers of grace until the very power to receive
> grace perishes.[6]

Some of the great tragedies of world literature have centred around just this theme. One thinks of Dr Faustus, in Marlowe's tragedy of that title, coming

---

[5] Berkouwer, op. cit., p. 348.
[6] Plummer, pp. 122–123.

to realize the irreversibility of his fate, and crying out, 'My heart's so hardened I cannot repent.' There can hardly be a greater human tragedy.

John's concern, therefore, is that his 'dear children' shall not be led into apostasy by the heretical teachers, whose denial of Christ's deity and his atoning work meant that they were self-condemned to eternal death. But could it be possible for a true believer (a *brother or sister*, 16) to be so deceived and actually to lose his or her salvation? Does this not conflict with the biblical teaching, usually called 'the perseverance of the saints', that salvation is an eternal work of God's grace and that once we are in Christ we are in him for ever?

Verse 16 speaks of a *brother or sister* committing *a sin that does not lead to death*. There is nothing about a Christian believer committing the sin that leads to death; simply the reminder that such a sin does exist. So the first part of verse 16 is relevant to church life, in every congregation and every generation, and is part of the assurance in prayer God wants all his people to have. It is an instruction about what is sadly a common event in church life. A Christian becomes enmeshed in some sin which becomes obvious to a fellow Christian. That Christian's privilege and responsibility is to pray for the erring brother or sister, with confidence and faith that he or she will be given life, and be restored to that full fellowship with God which is eternal life and which any and every sin spoils and mars.

The subject of the verb *will give* (*God will give them life*) is sometimes questioned, as the construction could point to the intercessor as the giver by virtue of his or her prayer. In agreement, however, with the weight of Scripture that God alone is the giver of life (and this is an emphasis in John's Gospel – see 6:35; 10:28; 17:2) it seems that the NIV and other translations are more than justified in inserting 'God' as the subject.

So the sinning Christian, whose life in Christ is declining, though he or she is not dead nor sinning unto death, will be restored, by the grace of God, through the prayers of the Christian church family. That Christian will be convicted by the Holy Spirit whom he or she has been grieving or quenching, brought to a renewed repentance and faith, and restored to walking in the light with God. This is a very great stimulus to the church to pray believingly for the full restoration of Christians who wander or 'backslide'. It is also an important duty, for as verse 17a reminds us, *All wrongdoing is sin*. Sin matters because it destroys fellowship with God and between Christians. 'But if anybody does sin, we have an advocate with the Father – Jesus Christ, the Righteous One' (2:1). And it is our task to speak to the same Father, through the Son, whenever we are aware that one of his children is wandering into sin. All the weight of the divine covenant commitment lies behind our expectation of faith that such a Christian will be restored. So we must pray with boldness and confidence.

But with regard to the sin that leads to death, John comments, *I am not saying that you should pray about that.* Several commentators point out that even in this extreme case the apostle is not forbidding prayer. He simply does not command or encourage it. The reasons which we have already examined are implicit in the nature of the sin. There is a hardening of the heart against God which, as Pharaoh found (Exod. 10:27), becomes irremediable when God confirms the individual's choice of death. Again, this is in harmony with what John has already written about the 'anti-christs', who 'went out from us, but . . . did not really belong to us' (2:18–23). Having denied the doctrines of salvation and left the community of God's faithful people, such apostates, whatever they may once have professed to believe, have put themselves beyond the reach of the church's prayers. These people cannot be true believers, whatever they may claim, for the essence of unbelief is to deny the Christ, whom Christians confess as Saviour and Lord. Although they may have been fully involved in the life of the church, they are revealed by their apostasy never to have really belonged. John is in agreement with Hebrews 6:4–6, that 'it is impossible' for them, 'who have fallen away, to be brought back to repentance. To their loss they are crucifying the Son of God all over again and subjecting him to public disgrace.' That is why John does not encourage prayer for such people.

2. A new antipathy towards sin (5:18)

Verse 18 and the next two verses each begin with a shout of confidence, *We know.* They continue with a closing emphasis on some of the great assurances that have already been expounded more fully elsewhere in the letter. Here is true knowledge, which is the birthright of the humblest Christian by the Spirit through God's Word, as compared with the spurious theorizing of the false teachers which is based solely on their own inflated egos and ingenious imaginations. These are things true believers know 'from the beginning' and from which they need never be shaken.

Christians do not go on sinning. This is ground we have travelled over before (2:29; 3:6, 9) and it should be a foundational certainty in the practical, ethical outworking of our faith. It is an uncompromising statement, inclusive of every true believer in Jesus (*anyone born of God*). By now, we know better than to say that if we sin this verse means that we cannot be truly born of God. The letter does not promise or encourage perfectionism, as we have often commented. Nor does it say that this is a special level of super-spirituality or holiness available only to the favoured few. No Christians go on sinning as they did before they turned to Christ. The reason is that *the One who was born of God keeps them safe.*

Some confusion has arisen here by taking the two uses of the English phrase *born of God* in this verse to be identical. Such a view places the onus on born-again Christians to keep themselves safe and immune from evil. It would lead many of us to despair as we come to realize increasingly how deeply ingrained sin is within our very nature. There would be little cause for confidence if our victory over sin was dependent on our own ability to keep ourselves safe. But in the original the phrases are not identical. The first is the perfect participle (*gegennēmenos*), which John regularly uses to describe Christians. It indicates a relationship begun at a point in the past with a continuing effect in the present. Because I was born, I am alive now. That is true both naturally and spiritually. The second use, however, is the aorist participle (*gennētheis*), which expresses a once-for-all fact. It refers to the one who was always born of God, outside of time, and who is therefore the eternal Son. The NEB actually translates, 'it is the Son of God who keeps him safe'. How is a Christian delivered from continuing in sin? Not by that Christian's own efforts (though certainly he or she has to appropriate God's resources and cooperate with God's grace), but by the life of the eternal Son, planted in the soil of the Christian's redeemed human personality.

It is Christ who keeps God's children safe, so that Satan cannot, literally, 'fasten himself' upon them. He may and will attack God's children, but he cannot gain a foothold; he cannot succeed in getting them back into his grip. That is where the world is, as verse 19 will show us – in the grip of the evil one. But the church is kept safe by the eternal Son, to whom all power is given and who guarantees, in his own words, her total security.

I give [my sheep] eternal life, and they shall never perish; no one will snatch them out of my hand. My Father, who has given them to me, is greater than all; no one can snatch them out of my Father's hand. I and the Father are one.
(John 10:28–30)

So, as we struggle against sin in our lives, we do so with confidence, not despair. Our protector is stronger than our enemy; more vigilant and more concerned than we can ever be. We know it is true, so let us rejoice in it and live in the experience of it, by faith. Could anyone express this humble certainty more persuasively and powerfully than Toplady in his hymn?

> A sovereign Protector I have,
>   Unseen, yet for ever at hand,
> Unchangeably faithful to save,
>   Almighty to rule and command.
> He smiles, and my comforts abound;
>   His grace as the dew shall descend;
> And walls of salvation surround
>   The soul he delights to defend.[7]

3. A new attitude to the world (5:19)

Christians know that they belong to God and not to this world. John's second great affirmation focuses first on the personal relationship that exists between God's children and their Father. Literally, 'we know that we are of God'; the construction stresses that God alone is the source of our life. This explains and justifies the NIV's inclusion of the word *children*. All that we have comes from him and so we belong to him totally: body, mind and spirit. That is something a Christian knows, not presumptuously, but because of the positive evidences in life and behaviour of the new birth, as John's letter has outlined and described them. By definition, then, God's family is separated out from *the whole world*. Children of God live differently from the non-Christian society surrounding them.

It is a matter of lordship. The world is *under the control of the evil one*. It is dominated by the devil, who controls it with tyrannical authority, organizing and orchestrating its life and activities to express his own rebellion and hatred against God. You have only to read today's newspaper or listen to the next news bulletin to know that that is true. In contrast, God controls his children in a rule of light and love, so that they offer no allegiance to this world. Of course, we also need to remember that the

---

[7] Augustus Montague Toplady (1740–78).

devil is a creature, subject to God's authority, who is not allowed to go an inch further than God's permission sanctions (see Job 1 – 2), and whose ultimate doom is assured (Rev. 20:10). That is why the world's freedom is slavery, and the devil's offer of autonomy from God, which lies at the root of all sin, an illusion.

All the major compulsions of twenty-first-century living – alcohol, sex, drugs, gambling, social media – are in fact attempts to escape from the slavery of sin into a world of personal fulfilment and satisfaction. But the raging thirst of men and women without God confirms that such short-term, selfish means of 'satisfaction' are like drinking salt water. The more you have, the more you want; the more you want, the less you are satisfied. That is always the devil's way.

And what is true at the individual level is becoming frighteningly true at the international and global level, not only politically and militarily, but ecologically too. The tyranny of sin is selfishness. It is self-love that opposes true love. Thoughtful and concerned people articulate the problems, but the world is not free to solve them. It lies in the destroyer's grip. Sir Peter Scott, the naturalist and conservationist, suggested that we need an 'ombudsman for generations unborn' to try to head off their doomed inheritance of a dying planet. 'I think that vast disasters will overtake mankind unless we all look further into the future than we do at the moment and put long-term benefit above short-term advantage.'[8] But that requires a moral courage and ability which humankind does not have.

Christians *know* that these things are so, and they know why. What is inexcusable is for the church to concentrate on trying to preserve its distinctives in a hermetically sealed environment of detachment from the world and its problems. That is a luxury Christ has not afforded us. Indeed, it is not a luxury at all, but a quick route to death by suffocation. If we live under Christ's lordship we must remember that he has commissioned us all to go into the world, not to withdraw from it. Our new attitude is not one of indifference or separation, but one of involvement and compassion, after the model of our Saviour. If these things are certainties in our thinking, they must be seen in our commitment to being salt and light in our communities, and above all to communicating the gospel of Jesus Christ. In the words of Jude, 'Keep yourselves in God's love as you wait for the mercy of our Lord Jesus Christ to bring you to

---

[8] Sir Peter Scott in a speech to the Law Society, reported in *The Times*, 9 October 1976.

eternal life. Be merciful to those who doubt; save others by snatching them from the fire' (Jude 21–23).

4. A new awareness of God (5:20–21)

This last great conviction is of course the ground and substance of the preceding two: We know . . . that the Son of God has come . . . so that we may know him . . . And we are in him. Our victorious faith is grounded in what God has done in history, in Christ. Christians know that 'Jesus Christ has come in the flesh' (4:2), and that he came 'by water and blood' (5:6). His coming has given us understanding, which seems to be both a spiritual and an intellectual capacity to receive truth. God's truth is addressed to the mind, through which it penetrates the heart, to activate the will; but it is not primarily understood intellectually. There is always a further moral, spiritual aspect involved. For understanding Christian truth is not a matter of mastering doctrinal formulations, important though they are, or of grasping abstract philosophical ideas like those the Gnostics propagated; but of meeting, knowing and submitting to the person who is truth, so that we may know him who is true. This kind of knowledge becomes fellowship. For Jesus the Son came to bring us into a personal relationship with God. True Christians can be sure, therefore, that their mind has been illuminated and their will motivated by the Holy Spirit of truth, who has revealed Jesus as the true Son of God and through whom they have come to know the true God, who is eternal life.

And we are in him (20b). It is not only that Christ has revealed the Father by his incarnation, perfect life, atoning death and glorious resurrection, but that through all this he has brought us into the closest possible union with the one true God. By faith, we enter into a relationship that will never end. We are in God and he is in us, his people, so that in Christ we are as close as we possibly could be and God shares with us his own indestructible life, the life of the eternal. Here is reality, because here is Truth, ultimate and absolute. This is the fellowship with the Father and the Son which John introduced as the essence of eternal life at the very beginning of his letter (1:2–3). So we have come full circle. We have reached the top of the spiral staircase and found God himself, and in him everlasting life. And all our climbing has been with the explicit purpose that we might know that these things are objectively true, and real in our own personal experience. Christians do know that these things are true, and nothing need shake that assurance. For at its heart lies the unassailable fact that, by God's grace, we know him and are in him.

But it is not a call to luxuriate in a bubble bath of Christian assurance. *Dear children, keep yourselves from idols* (21). Here is the corollary – our responsibility – which matches the keeping power of the Lord Jesus (18). 'An idol is anything which occupies the place due to God.'[9] It is an imitation or substitute, rather than the reality. It may be made of wood, or stone, or precious metals. It may be carved and shaped by someone's hands. But it is unlikely that John was thinking of such artefacts. His concern was with the false ideas and heretical concepts of God to which the church was being subjected.

The warning is no less appropriate to us today. Some contemporary manifestations of idolatry are almost as crude as the images of the first century. Mammon is still a powerful deity, as people live for what they have or what they can acquire. In its more sophisticated forms, materialism becomes a quest for power, social status, success, fame. The world is full of self-made people who worship their creator, and the church is not immune to the temptations. We need to guard ourselves against them. But in our century, too, it is false ideas of God, cardboard cut-out substitutes for the living and true God, that invade and destroy our spiritual lives. Whether it is the 'demythologized' God of radical theology, shorn of his supernatural power, or the pocket-size God of evangelical overfamiliarity, deprived of his majesty, the danger is the same. We can all too easily think we have him sewn up, we know all about him, we can predict his responses and even condition them. But what we have is not God. It is an idol of our own making, a thinly veiled excuse for worshipping ourselves.

Keep yourselves from idols. Anything that squeezes God out of the central position towards the margin of my life must be ruthlessly toppled. Any notion of God which contradicts his perfect self-revelation in Jesus Christ must be rejected. This letter, indeed the whole Bible, was written to enable us to distinguish truth from error. We have a responsibility to attend to sound teaching, to guard our Christian lives, to have done with false goals, whether spiritual, intellectual or material. The enemy is still false teaching, inspired by the evil one; but Christians can be sure. They can know with certainty that they have eternal life. They can have confidence about the things that matter most.

---

[9] Westcott, p. 197.

2 John

19. Priorities of truth and love

The second and third letters of John (along with Philemon) are the nearest we approach, in the New Testament, to a conventional piece of first-century correspondence. Their length indicates that they were probably written on a single sheet of papyrus; their content, that they are dealing with a particular set of circumstances and therefore have a specific destination. The background is already familiar to us through our studies of John's first letter, and the major concerns or themes of this second letter remain the same – the priorities of *truth* and *love*.

The gospel was continuing to spread rapidly. House churches were springing up throughout the Graeco-Roman world. The apostolic writings were beginning to circulate among them, but the apostolic generation had all but died out. It seems more than likely that John was the only remaining member of the original group of twelve. The careful oversight of the church depicted in the Acts of the Apostles was no longer possible. At the same time travelling preachers and missionaries were increasing.

But the message did not always ring true to the gospel the apostles had preached. Some claimed new insights, taking them beyond the apostolic testimony, which was caricatured as primitive and unsophisticated. There was a fullness of knowledge and experience into which such teachers had been initiated and which they were willing to pass on to others, at a price. The temptation to join this self-defined spiritual elite must have proved very strong. Others wanted to go back to the Old Testament, to the purity of the law and the 'essentials', such as circumcision. This Judaizing tendency, though not as dangerous as the threat of Gnosticism, was not absent from the churches. The most pressing question, which clearly exercised John's mind and burdened his spirit, was how these young churches were to be kept strong in the true faith, and how they were to maintain their priorities with both unswerving orthodoxy and vigorous spiritual life. That is why these two short letters were inspired, written, and preserved within the New Testament canon.

But who is the author, and to whom is he writing? The nameless writer introduces himself simply as *the elder* (1). From the earliest times the letter has been attributed to John the apostle, but not without debate. The early evidence is sparse, though the Muratorian Canon, a fragmentary list of New Testament books known at Rome about AD 200, certainly includes the first two letters. Irenaeus, bishop of Lyons (*c*.175–*c*.195), quotes from 2 John, but Eusebius (*c*.265–*c*.339), in his *Ecclesiastical History*, mentions 2 and 3 John as books which were disputed by some but generally accepted in the church (a view expressed also by Origen and Jerome). Following a passage in Papias (*c*.60–130), bishop of Hierapolis in Phrygia, who was said to have heard the apostle John, several scholars have attributed the two short letters to 'John the presbyter (elder)' – a different person entirely.

Much depends on whether John the apostle might not also be known as 'the elder', and the scholarly debate continues on this issue.[1] The definite form of the title ('the elder') shows that it was quite sufficient to identify the author to his readers. Though *presbyteros* literally meant 'an old man', there can be little doubt that here 'it describes not age simply but official position'.[2] The apostle Peter was able to describe himself as 'a fellow elder' (1 Pet. 5:1) without any diminution of his apostolic authority, and there seems to be no conclusive reason why the apostle John may not have done the same, particularly at a time when, as an old man, he was the last remaining member of the apostolic band left on earth. For one whose relationship towards his readers is that of fatherly affection for his little children, it is a very appropriate title. Certainly the content and vocabulary of the three letters indicate one author behind them, which, F. F. Bruce comments, 'is, in my judgment, scarcely to be doubted'.[3] It must be added that the apostle John is by far the most likely candidate to fill that role.

What, then, of *the lady chosen* [elect] *by God and . . . her children*, to whom the elder is writing? Some have taken the addressee to be an

---

[1] For a full discussion, see Marshall, pp. 42–49.
[2] Westcott, p. 223.
[3] Bruce, p. 136.

individual named Kyria (lady or mistress), or the lady Electa (following Clement of Alexandria). Some older commentators, Plummer among them, regard her as a matriarch, perhaps a widow, ruling her family in the ways of the Lord. But most modern commentators (including Westcott, Lenski, Bruce and Marshall) opt for a corporate identity and see the destination of the letter as a local church, personified as a lady. Others (such as Bultmann) suggest the catholic or universal church; but the church in that sense has no *sister* (13).

It is one of the issues on which we cannot be thoroughly sure, but when we remember that *kyria* is the feminine form of *kyrios* (Lord) and that *chosen* is an adjective frequently applied to the church as the bride of Christ, it seems to make most sense to regard this letter as addressed to a church, whose members are the *children* of verses 1 and 4. This is made the more likely by the additional comments that *all who know the truth* love her, as the author himself does (1). For one of John's great themes is the mutual love that exists between Christians, whether individually or corporately. It seems unlikely that such a reference could be made about a single family unit, however well known; but it would certainly apply to a local church, in fellowship with others in its province or area.

In verse 1 John speaks of loving his readers *in the truth*, which could mean 'in reality' or 'genuinely', since there is no definite article in the Greek. Be that as it may, this leads John to expand on *the truth* (2), which is the foundation of all valid Christian fellowship. Knowledge of the truth as it is in Jesus Christ produces a deep bond of love between all who share it. As the first letter taught us, to know Christ is to love him, and to love Christ is to love all those who are united to him, through faith. But that special characteristic of mutual support and loving care among believers is rooted in the soil of truth. It is because Christ really is who he claimed to be that those who trust in him are transformed by that relationship. So John is already stressing that truth is primary for the Christian. It is not that members of the church are all of the same religious 'type', or that they are naturally drawn to one another by a common interest, as in a secular club. Christian unity is grounded in the truth alone, and the truth alone can generate *agapē* (that distinctive self-giving love), since it is both an internal force and an eternal reality. The truth *lives in us* (literally, it 'remains' or 'abides') when we realize what it is, believe it and practise it. Such an involvement of spiritual energy will yield an eternal dividend, for God's truth will never be outdated or eclipsed. It is instructive that here

John speaks about the Word in the same way that the Lord Jesus spoke to his disciples about the Spirit: 'he lives with you and will be in you' (John 14:17). Because 'the Spirit is the truth' (1 John 5:6) this is a natural equation to make. It serves to remind us how unbiblical and fruitless it is to seek to polarize the Word and the Spirit, or to opt for one or the other. The teaching which separates Word from Spirit, truth from love, mind from heart, doctrine from experience, destroys not only personal Christian integrity but the whole fabric of the apostolic testimony.

Verse 3 brings us to the greeting. Often this was no more than a word (see, e.g., Acts 23:26), but among Christians it was usually extended to include at least 'Grace and peace from God'. John's greeting is more of a benediction. Taking up verse 2, *the truth . . . will be with us*, he repeats the verb and introduces *grace, mercy and peace*, 'walking arm in arm with us'.[4] Grace (unmerited favour) begins in the heart of God, is expressed towards human beings in mercy, and is experienced by us as the bless- ing of peace. These three qualities can be comprehended in the word 'salvation' which describes most fully the reality in our experience, by which God gives us what we do not deserve (mercy) and does *not* give us what we do deserve (judgment). The channel through which grace, mercy and peace flow is *the Father's Son*, our Lord and Saviour Jesus Christ. So the truth of who Christ is and what he has done for us always exists side by side with the love we experience as we believe in him. The objective reality that the man Christ Jesus is the eternal Son of the Father, the only true God, undergirds our personal experience of that love in salvation and guarantees its eternal validity.

1. Priorities and how to live by them (4–6)

Not surprisingly *truth* is the first great priority, underlined even by the opening greetings. John's greatest *joy* is to find Christian disciples who are continuing steadfastly in *the truth*, children of God who are demonstrating the family likeness (4). As always, the Scriptures balance God's sovereignty with our responsibility. If it is a fact that 'the truth . . . lives in us . . . for ever' (2), it is the Christian's unavoidable duty to walk *in the truth* (4). There can be no option about this; it is the main ingredient of our discipleship. The truth of God, revealed supremely in the living Word, and

---

[4] Lenski, p. 559.

recorded unerringly in the written Word, provides the route by which the Christian is travelling from earth to heaven. This is the road we are to follow. If we want to make a journey we need to read the map and carry out its instructions; it is not a matter of choice. You cannot reach the north by travelling west.

But there is a stronger constraint, which John now introduces. We are to walk in the truth *just as the Father commanded us* (see 1 John 3:23). The danger was that only *some of* the *children* were following the right pathway (though perhaps John had not met all the church members). It seems likely that one of his reasons for writing is to correct a loose attitude to obedience to the truth, which was already infecting some members of the congregation.

The exhortation of verse 5 is therefore introduced against the background of both joy and anxiety expressed in verse 4. We are to remember and practise the commandment which is laid upon each believer at the outset of our spiritual experience – *I ask that we love one another*. Here is the other great biblical priority, always twinned with truth. The theme has been fully expounded in the first letter (see 1 John 2:7–11; 3:14–18; 4:12, 20–21) but it can hardly be reiterated too often. The God who calls us to believe also calls us to love. Both are equally vital. There is nothing new in that, though when the Lord Jesus first spoke in such terms, he described it as a new commandment (John 13:34). But by now it was well known as a central requirement of Christian devotion.

It is still well known today. The question is not whether we know it, but whether we do it (cf. John 13:17). Such love does not begin with the emotions so much as with the will. Yet as we set ourselves to work for the good of others, whatever the personal cost to ourselves, we so often find that feelings of concern and care develop into a real affection and love. The mark of Christian authenticity is to make that conscious decision of the will to give ourselves away in caring for one another. There is never a day in our lives when it does not need to be renewed and reaffirmed.

To *love* the Lord is to obey him in every detail of his will, expressed in his *commands* (6a). Some have accused John of arguing in a circle. Here he defines love as obedience, while in the preceding verse he has stated that the divine commandment is to love, which is repeated at the end of verse 6. It is worth noting that, in verses 5 and 6b, *command* is singular; walking in love is a summary of what it means to obey God. In verse 6a, *commands* is plural, since the outworking of love is a daily, disciplined concern to fulfil God's will as completely as possible. This is why the Lord Jesus himself, when asked, 'Of all the commandments, which is the most important?', responded, '"Love the Lord your God with all your heart and with all your soul and with all your mind and with all your strength" . . . "Love your neighbour as yourself." There is no commandment greater than these' (Mark 12:28–31).

On that basis, Paul concludes in Romans 13:10 that 'love is the fulfilment of the law'. Love and obedience to the truth are inseparable priorities if we are to live as God requires. And yet which of us, as Christians, does not find it a continual struggle to *walk* consistently, one step after another, along the path of obedience? Sometimes we separate obedience from love, so that it hardens into a grinding duty, a ritualistic keeping of the rules. It is hardly surprising that we eventually lose heart and give up the struggle. But if we are in a right relationship to God, if our Christianity is primarily a matter of love for God, we shall find, as John did, that 'his commands are not burdensome' (1 John 5:3). Love for the Father and the Son is the great incentive to obedience and to moving on in the narrow way of the truth.

But what if our love is weak and faint? How do we increase our capacity to love God? Again the first letter has answered the question. 'We love because he first loved us' (1 John 4:19). We go to the truth of God's Word, to the Bible, and soak ourselves in all that we see of God's being and character there, especially his great love for us. We go back to the cross where he showed his love most clearly and remember that 'the Son of God . . . loved me and gave himself for me' (Gal. 2:20). We constantly feed our minds and souls with the assurance that God could not possibly love us more than he does and that he will never love us less. 'I have loved you with an everlasting love; I have drawn you with unfailing kindness' (Jer. 31:3). He will never let us down. He will never let us go. He will never give us up. We may grieve him, through our sin, and in his love he will discipline us, as every loving father must (Heb. 12:10–11). The discipline may be painful, but even this is for our good. He never for one moment stops loving us.

We need to take some of the New Testament's great affirmations of that unfailing love, limitless grace and keeping power, and read ourselves into them, personally, by name. Passages like Romans 8:31–39, Ephesians 1:3–14 and 1 Peter 1:3–9 are medicine to the soul. When the love of God is not a present reality to us, we need to take that medicine, three times a day, after meals, until our spiritual appetite begins to pick up and we begin to respond in awe to God's overwhelming grace:

> Yet I may love thee, too, O Lord,
>   Almighty as thou art,
> For thou hast stooped to ask of me
>   The love of my poor heart.[5]

We obey the Lord because we love him, as the Lord. We love him because we feed our souls on the truth of his Word, which reveals his character and his great plan for the salvation of men and women. And as we believe and appropriate all that his Word promises – that eternal life which is ours by our union with Christ – so we grow in truth and love, receiving more and more his grace, mercy and peace. These are the divine priorities we are called to develop.

2. Problems and how to cope with them (7–11)

Although the NIV begins a new paragraph at verse 7, the verse actually begins with 'because'. That word is a link with all that John has written in verses 4–6. As we have seen, failure in love usually indicates a failure to know and practise the truth. One cannot suffer without the other suffering too, just as each will also strengthen the other. It is because of the crisis of truth which the church is facing, through the inroads of the *deceivers* with their false teaching, that John wants to stir his readers up to be more determined in their Christian love for one another. Love like that can be one of the church's strongest defences against heresy, just as holding to the truth is the greatest bastion against error.

a. How to resist false teaching

It is a fundamental principle of the New Testament writers not to devote themselves to the detailed dissection or even analysis of the false teaching they were combating. Rather, they give themselves to the positive proclamation of the truth, confident that it will, in and of itself, undermine and destroy the error.

---

[5] 'My God, How Wonderful Thou Art', by Frederick William Faber (1814–63).

The word *deceivers* (*planoi*) is related to a verbal root meaning 'to lead astray' or 'to cause to wander', the verb itself being used in 1 John 2:26. They have two primary characteristics by which they may be recognized: erroneous belief and erroneous behaviour.

First, they *do not acknowledge Jesus Christ as coming in the flesh*. This is not a matter of private unbelief, but of public denial. They actively teach that he did not come in the flesh.

Here, interestingly, John uses the present participle (*as coming*) whereas in 1 John 4:2, in a similar context, he used the perfect ('has come'). The present seems to underline the fact that God is still incarnate in Jesus. Some false teachers, such as Cerinthus, were quite prepared to acknowledge and teach that the Christ descended upon the human Jesus at his baptism, but they believed this visitation to have ended before the cross, since God could not, and did not, suffer and die. What John wants to establish is that the Word, which once became flesh, is still flesh and always will be; that the Christ who has ascended to the majesty of the Father is, at one and the same time, the human Jesus. There is a glorified man in heaven. The effect of the deceivers' teaching was to deny that the divine and human natures were united in the one person within the womb of the virgin Mary, never to be separated. Anyone making such a denial is *antichrist*, because it strikes at the very basis of Christ's person and work, on which the Christian faith is built.

Second, they *have gone out into the world*. There are two possible meanings here. We may be meant to understand that they have 'gone out' as missionaries do, penetrating new areas with the gospel. If that is right, the false teachers were spreading their heresies with missionary zeal, eager to influence new areas and dominate other churches. The prophecy of Jesus that 'false messiahs and false prophets will appear and perform signs and wonders to deceive, if possible, even the elect' (Mark 13:22) was being fulfilled, and his earlier warning, 'Watch out that no one deceives you' (Mark 13:5), was very much to the point. In fact, John reiterates it in verse 8.

On the other hand, John normally uses *kosmos* to mean the non-Christian world, organized in opposition to God's rule (see 1 John 2:15–19). If that is his meaning here, he is reminding us that one of the marks of false teachers is their secession from those who hold to orthodoxy. They cannot exist in the environment of truth, the faithful church, because they deny its essential doctrines. Whoever they are (*any such person*), and however attractive they may appear to be in person or presentation, they are enemies of Jesus, *antichrist*.

> Whatever it [*antichristos*] means elsewhere, here it is used to characterize people who are radically opposed to the true doctrine about Christ and are thus supremely his opponents, even if they protest that they hold the truth about him and are Christians. The elder says that anybody who denies the truth is a very antichrist, just as we might speak of a supremely evil person as 'the very devil'.[6]

In view of the seriousness with which John views the problem, it is not surprising to find the warning of verse 8 couched in strong terms: literally, 'Look to yourselves.' Complacency is always a danger, and nowhere more so than when error is being plausibly propagated by pleasant exponents. 'He's such a nice man; surely his views cannot be so wrong' is a common reaction still. But there are much larger issues at stake than individual personalities. There is the danger that those who embrace error will forfeit their reward. Textual readings vary here. The NIV adopts the first-person plural which may be the correct reading (*what we have worked for*). It certainly makes good sense. John would then be expressing his personal concern, as an apostle, that all the hard work of evangelism, teaching and pastoral care to which the church leaders of his generation had given themselves so sacrificially would in the end come to nothing if the church in the next generation turned away from the truth.

But it would not be only the leaders who would suffer loss; the readers would do so as well, if they were to embrace false teaching. There is a reward for faithful service (see Matt. 25:21, 23), and John wants his readers to receive their full pay. The word implies a proper remuneration for work conscientiously completed. Perhaps the fullest explanation of this theme is in 1 Corinthians 3:12–15, where Paul says that on the judgment day the fire of God will test the quality of our service for him. 'If what has been built survives, the builder will receive a reward' (14). Paul clearly states that it is not an individual's salvation that is at issue, for that is a matter of grace and not of works; but faithfulness will bring its own reward. Like John, he wants his readers to receive it fully. If ever we are tempted to think that matters of truth and error are marginal, we should correct our

---

[6] Marshall, p. 71.

thinking by remembering the eternal perspective in which all our work and witness are carried on.

Verse 9 provides both a summing-up and a reiteration of the basic principles on which we are to judge this issue of truth. At the same time it underlines why failure to remain in the truth inevitably has such devastating spiritual consequences. Novelty is always deceptively attractive, and false doctrine can thrive where it is promoted as progressive, advanced thinking. It was characteristic of the pagan philosophers of Athens that they 'spent their time doing nothing but talking about and listening to the latest ideas' (Acts 17:21). They would have been very much at home in the chat shows and feature columns of our contemporary mass media. New ideas have an irresistible fascination for most of us. Wasn't that the angle from which the devil first approached Eve (Gen. 3:1–6)?

Now of course our instinctive quest for the new has led to incalculable benefits for our lives on this planet. The creation mandate to 'fill the earth and subdue it' (Gen. 1:28) can be viewed as God presenting humankind with Planet Earth as a puzzle of infinite complexity to unravel, a storehouse of vast riches to explore and utilize. So much of our quality of life which we take for granted in the twenty-first-century Western world derives from the courage, skill and sheer inquisitiveness of past generations. Yet it has also to be confessed that the mandate could be effectively fulfilled by humanity only under God's authority, as his vice-regent. Our new ideas have often proved to be 'thinking God's thoughts after him'. The danger comes when we imagine ourselves to be moving ahead of God, to have pressed on so far that we no longer need him. Then our new ideas become fantasy images which bear no relationship to reality as God has determined and constructed it. For as soon as we leave the basis of God's revealed truth, we begin to venture into unreality.

Sadly, many Christians have reacted against this by embracing what can only be called traditionalism for its own sake. They have allowed themselves to become stuck in a rut of backward-looking negativism, which is just as unbalanced as the pursuit of novelty. As a result, the Christian faith is caricatured by many as a cultural dinosaur, fossilized by layers of philosophical and ideological fashion, forever outdated and therefore irrelevant. Instead of proclaiming the unchanging truth of God in Christ as the only ultimate reality, the church has too often been sidetracked into a hopeless fight to preserve its own social and religious conventions. As with the Pharisees, so today, those who have (on paper at least) a very high view of the inspiration and authority of Scripture have often succumbed to the temptation to let go of the commands of God and hold on to human traditions (see Mark 7:8). Neither new ideas nor traditions are right or wrong in themselves. They all have to be brought to Scripture to be tested by its plumb line. There will always be a swinging pendulum of fashion in ideas and behaviour patterns, both in the world and in the church placed in that world by the Lord (John 17:15). Our responsibility is to discover the biblical perpendicular and to judge both the new and the old by its unchanging truth. To desert the doctrine of Christ is not progress but apostasy.

The Christian's responsibility, then, is to continue in that teaching. It is the *teaching of Christ*, not only in the sense that he is its centre and substance, but especially that it is the teaching he himself brought and which was embodied in himself. This underlines again both that Jesus is a historical figure and that our faith is rooted in real events, carried out in space and time by God, and therefore eternally valid. To move beyond what Paul describes as 'the pattern of sound teaching' and 'the good deposit' (2 Tim. 1:13–14) is quite simply to forfeit God. The logic is spelt out in verse 9. The only way to *have God*, that is, to have a personal relationship with God, is through faith in Jesus Christ, the Son. But those who deny his coming in the flesh cannot enter the only way to the Father (Jesus the Son), and so, whatever they may claim, they cannot have a genuine relationship with God. The Father and the Son are inseparable, one God for ever. The popular hymn is right when it exhorts us to 'come to the Father, through Jesus the Son'.[7] There is no other route. So the corollary is also gloriously true: that those who do believe the doctrine of Christ enjoy a living spiritual fellowship with both the Father and the Son (cf. 1 John 1:3).

b. How to relate to false teachers

Having dealt with the problem regarding truth with such clarity, John now focuses on those who actively propagate false teaching (10–11). This raises a problem of how to show love. Travelling prophets and preachers were multiplying in numbers, and Christians were well aware of their duty to give hospitality and support to God's messengers. John stresses, however, that this sort of practical encouragement must depend upon the content

---

[7] 'To God Be the Glory', by Fanny J. Crosby (1820–1915).

of the traveller's message. Verse 10 mentions two normal responses which Christian love would demand, especially towards those who devoted themselves full-time to an itinerant teaching ministry and were therefore dependent on the generosity of fellow Christians for board and lodgings. In love, Christians would take the visitors into their houses and give them a welcome. That this was an established pattern is confirmed by the instructions in the *Didache*, or *The Teaching of the Lord to the Gentiles through the Twelve Apostles*, a manual on church order, written in Greek, and probably dating from the early second century:

> Let everyone that cometh in the name of the Lord be received, and then, when you have proved him, you shall know, for you shall have understanding (to distinguish) between the right hand and the left. If he that cometh is a passer-by, succour him as far as you can; but he shall not abide with you longer than two or three days unless there be necessity.

By contrast, 'if the teacher himself is perverse and teaches another doctrine to destroy these things [i.e. apostolic doctrine], hear him not'.[8] Everything depends on the content of the message, not the plausibility or impecuniousness of the messenger.

Probably, in this verse we should think of the messenger as being welcomed into the church, rather than into an individual's home. It is less likely that the travelling teachers would be involved in door-to-door work than that they would arrive at a church meeting and ask to speak or participate in open worship. Of course, the church would be meeting in a house. To take the stranger in would therefore mean to accept the teaching and to welcome the stranger into the fellowship of the church. To *welcome* would similarly imply more than a formal politeness or recognition. It would be to express delight, to foster friendship. But if that sort of behaviour is extended to false teachers, it is not so much Christian love as spiritual suicide. It does not show love to the rest of the flock, because it exposes them to heresy's insidious undermining of their faith. It does not even show love towards the 'deceiver', since it simply confirms the error, which the stranger might now never be brought to admit. Above all, it does not express love for God, because it sides with evil in actively encouraging the spread of that which is most destructive of the truth (11).

---

[8] Quoted in *A New Eusebius*, ed. J. Stevenson (SPCK, 1957), p. 128.

The practical implications for us today are not difficult to draw, but they need to be carefully applied, remembering that the local church context is primary. These verses do not justify an individual in a spirit of sectarian separatism, which seems so often to have marred an otherwise faithful and fruitful life. The grounds of separation, as of unity, are the great central doctrines of the faith, not secondary matters of church order or government, on which Christian opinions will always differ. That there is a place for separation from those who deny the deity of our Lord Jesus Christ is undeniable. It is no part of Christian love for a church to welcome into its pulpit anyone who denies the teaching of Christ. Nor can different congregations or groups of Christians join together in 'evangelism' if the message to be proclaimed is not faithful to Scripture and agreed and preached by all concerned.

Equally, those who are united in the biblical gospel have a responsibility to demonstrate that unity by breaking down the barriers that separate them, whether denominational, cultural or traditional. They will agree to differ in those secondary matters on which Scripture is not black and white, respecting one another's right to hold a particular interpretation with conviction. They will not erect extra-biblical barriers to fellowship, nor will they allow their secondary differences to destroy their primary unity. Above all they will love one another and seek by all means to cultivate that love, so that the world will know whose disciples they are (see John 13:35).

But what should we do when we open our front door and discover there a member of one of the sects who has come to share with us 'another gospel'? Should we shut the door, or invite that person in? It is true that some who have later been converted to Christ from such groups have stated that they were snubbed by evangelical Christians more often than by others. Such bad manners and harshness are always inexcusable. It is possible to refuse to be involved in a conversation, but to do so politely and graciously (Col. 4:6). But it is also true that young and untaught Christians have often got themselves enmeshed in considerable difficulties by their misplaced generosity. Several commentators point to the example of Jesus eating with 'tax collectors and sinners' and being misunderstood, preferring this as the path to follow rather than a literal observance of verse 10. But the 'tax collectors and sinners' were not propagandists of false teaching which is ultimately parasitic on true Christianity, as many of today's cultists are. Perhaps Jesus' eating in the house of Simon the

Pharisee would be a closer parallel (Luke 7:36ff.). These verses do not preclude mature Christians from inviting a door-caller into the home in order to explain the error of those ideas held and the biblical truth and to seek, in love, to point the stranger to Christ. But Howard Marshall brings out the real point when he writes: 'There is a difference between giving a person love and even hospitality and providing him with a base for his work.'[9]

The closing two verses illustrate in two further practical ways how problems of truth and love in church life are always to be dealt with in love and truth. There is always more to be said than can readily be expressed on paper, however ready the writer. We cannot be sure what the many things John wanted to communicate were, though his other letters may fill in some of the gaps. Perhaps they were more personal matters affecting individuals within the church. We know from 3 John 10 that rebuke and correction may well have been foremost in the apostle's thinking.

But whether it is teaching, rebuking, correcting or encouraging, there is much to be said for doing it *face to face* (12), or literally 'mouth to mouth', as God spoke to Moses (Num. 12:8). The paper cannot smile, nor can it respond to changes of mood. Perhaps John was simply coming to the end of his single sheet of papyrus and did not want to start another. But a *visit* was what he was really looking forward to. His coming to strengthen the church and encourage their faith will *complete*, or 'fill full', their mutual *joy*. It is undoubtedly true, in experience, that open fellowship and Christian joy are best maintained and developed by personal, face-to-face contact wherever possible. Some of us too easily hide behind a letter, or even a phone call, when we should speak the truth in love in a personal meeting.

The letter ends with greetings from *the children of* the 'chosen lady's' 'chosen sister' (13). The fact that it is the children who send their greetings would tend to confirm our earlier interpretation of the 'lady' as a local church, and so of her *sister* as another local church with whom she was in fellowship. If this is accepted, then it reminds us that we exercise our love and hold to the truth in fellowship with all true congregations of God's people. It corrects isolationism, which can so easily develop into arrogance, in a church. We belong to a worldwide communion, and each church, locally, denominationally and nationally, needs her 'chosen

---

[9] Marshall, p. 75.

sisters' to help her see her own blind spots. We all have so much to learn from other Christians who hold the same truth and seek to exercise the same love as we do. We are all children of the same Father, members of the same family. The more we can live together in truth and love, the more will that climate be produced in which, together, our obedience to the Head of the church can flourish.

3 John

20. Learning by example

This last of the three letters attributed to John is the most personal of them all. Its similarity in length to the second letter is probably due to the fact that it occupied a single sheet of papyrus, and in many other ways the two letters mirror each other. In both, the author simply presents himself as *the elder* (see my comments on 2 John 1). In both, he expresses a desire to visit the recipient personally in order to talk further through the issues raised by the letter (13–14; cf. 2 John 12). In both, he is concerned about travelling teachers and the attitude of the congregation towards them. But whereas 2 John is primarily a warning against welcoming 'deceivers', 3 John is a warning against rejecting those who are true fellow Christians and ambassadors of the gospel. It is the positive complement of the negative prohibitions of 2 John, reminding Gaius and his congregation that the possible abuse of hospitality by the heretics is not to become an excuse for failing to show hospitality to true and faithful Christian preachers.

These similarities of theme, vocabulary and structure have led Lenski to surmise that 'the two letters were probably written on the same day and were sent to the same place, the second to the congregation, the third to one of the members'.[1] It is certainly an attractive idea. If the false teachers were beginning to penetrate the churches, then it was only to be expected that those who were impressed by the new ideas would exercise their authority, whether formally recognized or by force of personality, to keep out the orthodox teachers and promote the 'deceivers'.

---

[1] Lenski, p. 577.

Clearly this was happening in Gaius's church. He had received the believers from John, who were true messengers of Christ, and had welcomed, supported and entertained them in love. But the church generally had not done so, although there were those who wanted to. Control seems to have been in the hands of Diotrephes, a dominant personality, who not only rejected John's messengers but also slandered the apostle himself. In contrast, John commends Demetrius. He was probably the carrier of the letter and another representative of John, sent with the apostle's word to the church, in an attempt to put things right before John himself visits. As the letter revolves around these three men, it is helpful to use each of them as a focal point for our exposition of the text.

1. Gaius – a Christian friend (1–8)

We can know with certainty no more about *Gaius* himself than the contents of this letter tell us. Others of the same name are mentioned in the New Testament, but it was a common Roman name, and there is no reason to suppose that this Gaius would be mentioned elsewhere. Although unknown to us, to John he was a *dear friend* (*agapētos*). He is addressed in this way no less than four times (1, 2, 5, 11). This is related to the distinctive Christian word for 'love': the love that God has for us and which he creates in each of his children, so that as we are united in the truth, we are bound together in a supernatural love. As we have so often seen, far more than an emotion, this is a fundamental attitude to life.

John follows this first use of the address by stressing *whom I love in the truth*. The pronoun *I* is in an emphatic position, perhaps because Gaius, in taking an unpopular minority stand in the church, was not greatly loved by the heretical party that was developing around Diotrephes. The commendation of the elder would be a considerable encouragement to him in such circumstances. Whether we translate *truth* with or without the definite article, it was the truth of God in Christ that had bound John and Gaius together in love, and that was absolutely genuine. Christian friendship, one of God's greatest gifts, expresses the divine love, grounded in truth.

Christian friendship is also concerned about the well-being of a brother or sister in every department of life (2). While it was, and still is, conventional to express good wishes to one's reader at the start of a letter, a Christian writing to a fellow believer can go beyond 'I hope', or 'I wish', to

I pray. And our prayers for our friends can cover every aspect of life. So John is concerned about his physical *health* as well as his general well-being. *That all may go well with you* translates a verb which more literally means 'to have a prosperous journey' (cf. Rom. 1:10), a good trip, as we might say. There is no playing down of the physical essentials of life in the material world. Gaius is prospering spiritually, and John's concern is that his physical well-being will match the progress of his soul. The same verb is used (*euodoō*).

These passing comments are not only interesting in themselves, but instructive of the balance of physical and spiritual that characterizes the biblical outlook on life in the world. All too often, in church history, the pendulum has swung to one of the two extremes. Sometimes the emphasis has been on world negation, regarding the body as an encumbrance to the pure spirit, resulting in asceticism and self-mortification. This strand was there from the early church onwards, tending to lead its adherents into increasing legalism. 'Such regulations ['Do not handle! Do not taste! Do not touch!'] indeed have an appearance of wisdom, with their self-imposed worship, their false humility and their harsh treatment of the body, but they lack any value in restraining sensual indulgence,' Paul warned in Colossians 2:23.

At other times, the emphasis has been on identification with the world and acceptance of God's good gifts. But this also has been distorted, either towards licence, or towards the teaching which promises that every Christian should be infinitely healthy, wealthy and wise. But Christians are not automatically promised health and success. They are things to pray for, but they are dependent on a loving heavenly Father's perfect wisdom and sovereign rule. Physical prosperity is not a measure of spiritual health, nor is its absence a hindrance to spiritual progress.

There is no biblical wedge driven between the physical and the spiritual. We are 'in the body'. That matters, because it is how God has ordained things, and we know, therefore, that he is concerned about our physical well-being in his material world. There is no profit in pretending that we can live on a super-spiritual plane, when God has made us flesh and blood. Our attitude to life in this world should be positive, expecting God to be good and gracious to us because we know that is his character, but never for one moment presuming on his kindness, or imagining that this world is more important or significant than the next. It is sad, though, that some Christians seem to have allowed the devil to trap them into living under a cloud, so that they are always expecting some great disaster. If they are well and successful at present, you cannot expect that to last. If they are ill and discouraged, that just goes to prove how right they were. One cannot help feeling that such negativism dishonours the God of grace and mercy, to whom they belong, body and soul.

John's main concern is, however, with the spiritual health of Gaius, which he defines in two thoroughly characteristic ways. He is a man who shows *faithfulness to the truth* (3–4) and is *faithful* in his *love* for *the brothers and sisters* (5–8). After our studies in John's letters we would not expect any other criteria. Some of the travelling believers had been entertained by Gaius and had reported back to John his *faithfulness to the truth*. This was of course demonstrated by his love, in the generosity of his hospitality and his warm welcome. Truth and love are inseparable where they are genuine. Gaius was a man whose whole life was shaped by God's truth. Not only did he faithfully believe it, he continually practised it. There is no greater spiritual prosperity than that. His life was all of a piece. The things he believed, he lived out. So, whenever Christian strangers arrived, Gaius was ready to meet them and to welcome them. Nothing had to be changed. No special efforts had to be made. Those who were with him for only a short time could not fail to be encouraged by his faithful, consistent integrity, as a Christian.

Such news is the source of John's greatest *joy* (4), which is itself a comment on the writer's own spiritual maturity and devotion. Pastors' hearts are always most warmed and thrilled when they see spiritual progress in those under their care. Whether Gaius was a convert of John and so one of his *children* in that special sense, or whether the term is used simply of the next generation by an elderly man, we do not know, but there is no doubt about where the writer's heart lay – in encouraging maturity in the disciples known to him. Perhaps we should be challenged here at both levels. What would another Christian find if he or she came as your house guest? (As we answer that we need to remember that Jesus is with us at home every day.) And what gives you most joy in life? Is it to see others who are faithful to the truth, growing up in Christ?

This leads to the second commendation of Gaius: that he was also *faithful* in Christian *love* (5–8). The emphasis is not on verbal profession, but practical actions. Moreover, the present tense in verse 5 indicates that this attitude of open generosity is continuing and that John is counting on Gaius to go on with the good work. This is probably the immediate reason behind the writing of the letter, since it must have been very discouraging for Gaius continually to meet the hostility of Diotrephes and apparently to be in the minority in the church. He was unlikely to swerve from the faith, but he might well 'become weary in doing good' (Gal. 6:9). John wants to inspire in him the determination not to give up. He encourages Gaius by recounting the enthusiastic report about his faithful generosity to the travellers who had visited him (6a), even though he had not known them personally. Such past praise is the prelude to John's request (*Please send them on their way*) to continue his help and support for all the travelling teachers. Doubtless this would include not only food and accommodation while they were with him, but also the provision of money or supplies to help them on their way when they left.

And this was to be done *in a manner that honours God!* There could not be a higher standard of generosity to emulate. But then there could not be a higher or more worthy service than theirs. *It was for the sake of the Name that they went out* (7a). F. F. Bruce points out that this letter is the only New Testament document which does not mention Christ by name,[2] but that does not mean that he is not mentioned. Clearly, *the Name* in which they went, and in which Gaius so readily received them, was that of the Lord Jesus Christ, the only name in which salvation can be found (Acts 4:12), the name that is above every other name, at which every knee shall bow (Phil. 2:9–10). The early church used 'the Name' as a synonym for Christ (see Acts 5:41), encompassing within that the Hebrew tradition that the name expresses the nature. Indeed, when the Name is fully written it is 'in essence the sum of the Christian creed (cf. 1 Cor 12:3; Rom. 10:9)'.[3]

Verse 7 provides a necessary reminder of the motivation and intention of all Christian service. Their going out as missionaries obviously had an evangelistic purpose, as the reference to *the pagans*, or Gentiles, at the end of the verse demonstrates. But the making of disciples is never separable, biblically, from the maturing of those disciples, so that their work as teachers doubtless ran hand in hand with their gospel preaching. 'Teaching-evangelism', as it is sometimes called, was after all the New Testament norm, as the Acts of the Apostles makes clear.

Like Paul, these ambassadors of the Name did not expect financial support from the non-Christians to whom they went (cf. 1 Cor. 9:15–18).

---

2 Bruce, p. 150.
3 Westcott, p. 239.

Following the apostolic example, they did not want to be classed with the itinerant philosophers and religious experts, who made a good living from those who bought their knowledge and services. 'Freely you have received; freely give' was the principle the Master had taught (Matt. 10:8). But it is just that principle that imposes upon the church the obligation to support its missionaries. *We ought therefore to show hospitality to such people* (8a). And lest Gaius should find this too onerous a duty, John reminds him that it is also a privilege, *so that we may work together for the truth* (8b). Obviously it would call their message into question, at the very least, if they were not supported by those who claimed to believe the same things and whose lives were supposed to have been transformed by the good news. What sort of confidence could their hearers have if the devotees of this new teaching were not even prepared to stand by those who propagated it? Every Christian has a responsibility to work for the cause of the truth, and the extent to which we are prepared to do so, whatever it may cost us, may well be the most reliable indicator of the true depth of our believing. One of the greatest joys of Christian dedication is Christian teamwork.

It is significant that the major New Testament motivation for evangelism is not concern for the lost, but obedience to Jesus. We do not need to wait for a 'call' to be involved in the work of making Christ known, since the Great Commission, 'go and make disciples of all nations . . . teaching them to obey everything I have commanded you', remains unrescinded 'to the very end of the age' (Matt. 28:19–20). It is obedience to the dominical authority of Jesus that justifies Christian mission and must ultimately motivate us, not merely response to the needs of the world. Of course those needs stir us, even overwhelm us, but we do not let the world write the agenda, either for the church, or in our stewardship of the individual lives God has given us. We are Christ's servants first. As Paul expressed it, 'what we preach is not ourselves, but Jesus Christ as Lord, and ourselves as your servants for Jesus' sake' (2 Cor. 4:5). In serving the needs of the dying world we are primarily serving the Lord Jesus Christ (1 Cor. 15:58; Col. 3:23–24).

That being so, the whole church is the serving body, different members being differently gifted and fulfilling different functions, but all under the authority of the Head, whose will is sovereign. While some may be 'sent out', others will be required to support them. Christian workers are not to be vagrants, since this brings dishonour on the Name in which they go. Their Lord is the most gracious and generous of givers and it brings no credit to him if his ambassadors are impoverished because of the lack of generosity among their 'supporters'. It is not for nothing that the joke was made about the deacons' prayer for their minister, 'Lord, you keep him humble; we'll keep him poor.' Sadly, that attitude has often prevailed in the churches, where attention has centred on the minimum needed to get by, rather than on supporting the full-time servant *in a manner that honours God*. There are encouraging signs that biblical realism is beginning to prevail, and some of us in ministry are privileged to be on the receiving end of very generous material provisions.

But it still remains true that very few churches have cause for satisfaction when they look at their level of support for world mission, or even for their own missionaries. One still hears of missionaries who are able to stay on location abroad only with the financial support of their fellow missionaries. If local church leaders are to be held 'in the highest regard in love because of their work' (1 Thess. 5:13), surely that applies even more strongly in the case of those who have left home and family for the sake of the Lord and the gospel. Providing for the financial needs of those who have been sent out for the sake of the Name is a spiritual work in itself. Those who represent the Lord should be supported worthily, not in luxury but adequately. Some churches need to take these principles much more seriously.

As we remember that 'God loves a cheerful giver' (2 Cor. 9:7), let us also realize the great part that hospitality can play in forwarding the cause of the truth. In my own church, I can think of numerous people who have been integrated into the family because Christians gladly opened their homes to them, welcomed them, strengthened their faith and showed them genuine love. The descendants of Gaius are still with us, but we need many more who will *work together for the truth*.

2. Diotrephes – a Christian fraud (9–10)

John now moves into the major thrust of his short letter, which is to expose to Gaius the false motives and sub-Christian behaviour of *Diotrephes*, who was clearly exercising a great deal of influence in the church. John speaks of having already written *to the church*. Though Lenski asserts boldly, 'This is Second John,'[4] few commentators would agree with him, since

---

[4] Lenski, p. 584.

there is nothing explicit in that letter to relate it to this problem. It seems more likely that John had made another approach to the church, which Diotrephes had rejected. In such circumstances it would be surprising if the letter had survived. This third letter would then be another attempt by John to reach the church and to seek to persuade them to mend their ways, this time using Gaius as the channel.

There has been much discussion as to what lies behind John's brilliant cameo of Diotrephes, *who loves to be first*. Perhaps the RSV catches the meaning even more accurately: 'who likes to put himself first'. Was this a power struggle between a local church leader and an outside authority figure, John the elder or apostle? We have already noted that the expansion of the church and the death of the apostles combined to produce a period of considerable fluidity in the way in which the congregations were governed. Was Diotrephes one of the first local bishops, ruling the church and superior to the other elders?[5] Was he therefore striking a blow for the independence of the local congregation in resisting the elder's authority? There is no shortage of speculation on the subject. But what is certain is that his motives were all wrong. If he wanted the church to be autonomous, it was not for the church's benefit, but for the glory of his own ego. Above everything else, Diotrephes wanted to be in charge, and this all-consuming ambition had led him to break off relations with John. He refused to accept John's authority; he would not receive him in fellowship.

Verse 10 shows us that John and his group did not want peace at any price. Think of how Paul dealt with the Corinthians (e.g. 1 Cor. 4:18–21; 2 Cor. 13:1–4). Similarly, John is not prepared to allow the self-centred ambition of a man like Diotrephes to fester on unchecked. He is planning to visit the church soon and he will raise the matter when he comes, in order to bring it out into the open and to a satisfactory resolution.

Now we begin to see why. The motivating ambition which John has already censured is clearly illustrated by Diotrephes' malicious gossip. The verb (*phlyareō*) usually means 'babble incoherently', indicating that the accusations made were entirely without substance. It is characteristic of those whose only concern is for their own personal power to denigrate their opponents by any means possible. Because his heart was wrong, Diotrephes erred both from the truth and from Christian love. He began

---

[5] For a fuller discussion, see Bruce, pp. 152–153.

to spread untrue stories about John and refused to exercise the most elementary Christian grace of hospitality (*he even refuses to welcome other believers*) towards anyone who was associated with the elder. More than that, he prevented other members of the church from receiving John's messengers, and met all who dared to oppose him on this by excommunicating them from the church fellowship. Presumably Gaius was under the same threat.

Yet in all this, it is important to notice that nothing is said about Diotrephes actually welcoming false teachers, or being anything other than impeccably orthodox in his doctrinal stance. That may have played a part, but John does not draw attention to it. If the second and third letters were in fact written to the same church, we could assume that doctrinal deviation was a powerful factor in Diotrephes' behaviour. He would have kept out the true messengers presumably to let in the false. But we cannot establish that it was so, nor do we need to postulate gnostic influence behind his behaviour in order to understand it.

Diotrephes has had his followers throughout the history of the church, and the species is by no means extinct today. Too many congregations have been held in the grip of petty tyrants for us to regard this sad phenomenon as extraordinary. But the picture John draws of this domineering man is horrific. Destroying unity, flaunting authority, making up his own rules to safeguard his position, spreading lies about those whom he had designated his enemies, cutting off other Christians on suspicion of guilt by association – the catalogue is appalling. This is what happens when someone who loves to be first decides to use the church to satisfy an inner longing for a position of pre-eminence, for his or her own personal aggrandizement. We do not know whether or not Diotrephes had any official position, or whether he simply used the force of his personality to swing things his way. Either was possible and still is. There are churches today which are in the pocket of one person, or one family dynasty. Nothing can happen without the approval of X, because it is 'his' or 'her' church. Consequently, in effect, there can be no biblical plurality of eldership, no fresh or innovative ideas, no forward movement or spiritual growth. The Holy Spirit has long ago been drummed out of office in a church like that, where 'Diotrephes' rules. What a travesty of the Christian faith and family!

There is only one who can have pre-eminence in the church, and that is its Head, the Lord Jesus Christ. The true Christian leader is one whose life reflects John the Baptist's desire concerning his relationship with Jesus: 'He must become greater; I must become less' (John 3:30). Diotrephes clearly knew nothing of that, or of what it meant to be crucified with Christ, so his life was a fraud. Professing to be a Christian leader, he denied it by his words and actions; he usurped Christ's lordship of the church to feed his own ambition. The sentence Jesus himself pronounced on those who loved to have the most important seats in the synagogues and the places of honour, who devoured widows' houses and whose lengthy prayers were pious show, remains as a warning to the Diotrephes potentially within us all: 'These men will be punished most severely' (Mark 12:38–40). Whenever we start to serve ourselves rather than Christ, or to use our fellow Christians for our own ego trip, or to become concerned about our status within the church, we need to recognize the Diotrephes syndrome and take whatever strong action is needed to eliminate it. To behave as he did is neither faithful to the truth nor faithful to one's fellow Christians (3, 5).

3. Demetrius – a Christian follower (11–12)

Many commentators are surprised that John moves on from Diotrephes with an exhortation which seems quite mild, given the catalogue of Diotrephes' crimes against himself and the church. They have surmised that John must have been in a minority, or not sure of his ground, but Marshall's suggestion seems both more likely and more characteristic of the apostle: 'He was determined not to fight a battle of words and descend to his opponent's level.'[6] Verse 11 is typical of John's style, with its clear-cut antithesis between good and evil. That verb *imitate* bears witness to the way in which others' attitudes can colour and change our own, and to the speed with which they can permeate an entire congregation. If Diotrephes exemplifies what is *evil*, then Demetrius, in verse 12, will model what is *good*. Typically, John immediately connects the moral qualities of good and evil with an individual's personal relationship with God, or lack of it. Since what we call moral good is what is in harmony with God's will, and moral evil is what is at variance with it, John's unambiguously simple assertions follow logically. Those described as *from God* have been born of God and possess that

---

[6] Marshall, p. 91.

eternal life which is the power of God within a redeemed human personality. A life of goodness can be produced only by the life of God within. These things cannot be counterfeited. Similarly, those who persist in evil, whatever claims they may make to Christian experience or the knowledge of God, demonstrate by the absence of Christlikeness in their characters that they have *not seen God*. Gaius is urged to copy the good because by that lifestyle he proves the reality of his Christian profession.

But what does John mean by 'seeing God'? Clearly he is not referring to a mystical vision of God perceived in a state of heightened emotion or spiritual sensitivity. The Gospel which he wrote provides us with the answer. When Philip asked Jesus to show the disciples the Father, he received the reply, 'Don't you know me, Philip, even after I have been among you such a long time? Anyone who has seen me has seen the Father' (John 14:9). The same message is given at the conclusion of the Gospel's prologue: 'No one has ever seen God, but the one and only Son, who is himself God and is in the closest relationship with the Father, has made him known' (John 1:18). If anyone wants to see God, to know what he is like, the evidence is in Jesus, and he is the only means of contact. So we see God in Christ, the living Word, revealed to faith in the pages of the written Word. Those who do evil have not yet seen who God is or recognized the truth of Scripture. But when our spiritual eyes are opened we are brought into a saving relationship with God, through Jesus and the Word.

Demetrius is introduced (12) not so much to draw attention to him as a laudable individual (though he is that) as to underline that a genuine Christian life cannot remain hidden (cf. Matt. 5:14b). We cannot hide what we really are for long. Perhaps Demetrius was the messenger who carried John's letter to Gaius. Clearly he was well known as a Christian, and if John was writing from Ephesus it is tempting to conjecture whether he might not be the same Demetrius who had made silver shrines of Artemis and who had raised the uproar against Paul in the city, which had terminated his two-year ministry in the city (see Acts 19). If this man had been converted, many would have known about it and marvelled at his changed life. But we cannot say more than that it is possible.

The more difficult problem is to know what John means by saying he is well spoken of *even by the truth itself*. Bruce suggests 'that "the truth" is here personal, denoting our Lord (cf. John 14:6), and that we should translate "the Truth Himself"'.[7] Plummer prefers the explanation that 'the truth' is the Spirit of truth (cf. 1 John 5:6). On this view, the Spirit inspires and confirms the testimony of all those who know Demetrius (including John himself) to his integrity and thorough reliability.[8] So the Spirit stands behind the witnessing church enabling them to come to a right judgment. Another suggestion is that John means that the facts are self-explanatory and do not need any human support. But the most obvious meaning is that Demetrius lived his life according to God's Word of truth, so that when he was measured by that yardstick, the truth itself confirmed his quality. He was not found wanting.

Finally, John adds his own *testimony* in commending Demetrius to Gaius, so that the latter can have every confidence in receiving him as John's ambassador, whatever opposition Diotrephes may seek to stir up. If Demetrius was sent to prepare the way for John himself, then it was vital that he should be properly received, and everything depended on Gaius for that. So John draws upon his personal integrity and reliability, as well perhaps as his apostolic authority, to reinforce the dependability of his agent.

All that remains are the final thoughts and greetings. The similarity to 2 John is marked in verses 13–14a. Again John decides not to go into further detail *with pen and ink*. He much prefers to look forward to personal conversations with Gaius when he visits in the near future. The letter announces his imminent arrival, but it gives some time for those involved in the quarrels and disputes to think again and mend their ways. The dominant note is one of urgency, however, for the situation cannot be allowed to drag on.

Only the greetings follow. The first is conventional and yet warmly personal in the context of the letter. *Peace to you*, the familiar Jewish greeting, has a deepened significance when we remember the pressures Gaius was under and the state of war that seems to have existed in the church. But the peace that belongs to those who do what is good is a peace which the world can neither give nor take away. Together with the blessing of God's peace there is the blessing of Christian fellowship. Those who belong to the truth belong to one another. So *the friends* with John (probably Christians in Ephesus, perhaps those who had been so well received by Gaius)

---

[7] Bruce, p. 153.
[8] Plummer, p. 151.

send their best wishes, associating themselves with John's message and seeking to encourage Gaius by their support. Similarly, John asks that his personal greetings be passed on individually (*by name*) to those whom he knows with Gaius. This may have given his reader the opportunity to share the letter with the church; or, more likely, it underlines the fatherly concern John felt for the individuals he knew and loved, who were caught up in the squabbles and difficulties. It may well be a conscious echo of the only other use of the phrase 'by name' in the New Testament, on the lips of the Good Shepherd in John 10:3. That is the level of personal care and involvement the Good Shepherd has with each member of his flock, and John would not want to set for himself, as a pastor, any lesser target.

The early church was certainly not without its problems. Nor is its twenty-first-century equivalent. They are problems of our sinful human nature, which will be with us until Christ comes again – and yet every one of them could be met by God's superabundant grace. As we have looked at these three very different, and yet representative, church members around whom the letter revolves, we cannot fail to be challenged concerning our own discipleship. The ultimate proof of the truth we profess to believe and the love we profess to exercise will be seen neither in words nor in feelings but in the progressive transformation of our character, and therefore of our lifestyle, into the image of Christ.

The challenge to us now is how much we are really prepared to let Jesus Christ change us. Is it to be my will or his? On this will depend the ultimate verdict, whether we are proved to be frauds or followers. Who is at the centre of our lives? Is it 'self' with its longing to be first, to be number one? Or is it Christ, enabling us to keep faithful and to continue walking in the truth? There is still no issue with greater or more far-reaching implications for the church or for the Christian.

Study guide

It would be all too easy just to skim through John's letters without letting their truth take root in our lives. The purpose of this study guide is to help you genuinely to grapple with the message of the letters and to think how their teaching is relevant to you today.

Although designed primarily for Bible study groups to use over an eleven-week period, this series of studies is also suitable for private use. When used by a group with limited time, the leader should decide beforehand which questions to discuss during the meeting and which should be left for group members to work on by themselves during the following week.

To get the most out of the group meetings, each member of the group should read through the passage to be looked at in each study together with the relevant pages of this book. As you begin each session, pray that the Holy Spirit will bring these ancient letters to life and speak to you through them.

SESSION ONE

Ⓠ Introduction (pp. 1–8)

1 What do we know about the probable author of these letters? (See pp. 1–2.)

2 How is the moral background against which he wrote reflected in the letters? (See pp. 2–3.)

3 What were the main elements in the heresy John was writing to combat? What truths does he emphasize in consequence? How can we, two thousand years on, learn from this? (See pp. 3–7.)

4 David Jackman observes that we need to approach John's letters differently from Paul's. Why, and how? (See pp. 7–8.)

ⓠ 1 John 1:1–4
1. The prologue (pp. 9–15)

5 **Read verses 1–2.** What did John mean by the key phrase 'the Word of life'? How does it unlock the meaning of this unusual opening to the first letter? (See pp. 9–12.)

6 **Read verses 3–4.** Think of ways in which we often use the word 'fellowship' in Christian circles. According to these verses, how should we understand the word? (See pp. 12–15.)

SESSION TWO

ⓠ 1 John 1:5–7
2. Walking in God's light (pp. 16–21)

1 **Read verse 5.** How does David Jackman unpack the simple but profound statement that 'God is light'? (See pp. 16–19.)

2 **Read verses 6–7.** What three tests can we apply to those who claim to have fellowship with this God who is light? (See pp. 19–21.) What particular challenge or encouragement can you draw from David Jackman's exposition of these verses?

ⓠ 1 John 1:8–10
3. Radical treatment for sin (pp. 22–30)

3 **Read verse 8.** How would you explain the paradoxical fact that the more we walk in the light, the more we know ourselves to be sinners? What lies at the root of the teaching of some groups, then and now, that we can live 'without sin'? (See pp. 22–25.)

4 **Read verse 10.** What are some ways in which we today might try to deny that we have sinned? (See pp. 25–27.)

5 Verse 9 holds out the remedy for sin. What is implied by John's word 'confess'? (See pp. 27–28.)

6 In verse 9, John mentions two aspects of God's nature and two aspects of his response to our confession of sin. What are they? How do they assure us of forgiveness for our past and power for our future? (See pp. 28–30.)

SESSION THREE

(Q) 1 John 2:1–6
4. Marks of Christian reality (pp. 31–38)

1 What does David Jackman mean by 'Christian reality' or 'biblical reality'? (See pp. 31–32.)

2 **Read verse 1.** How does John describe Christ, and what do the terms mean? How do these truths enable us to be realistic about sin in our lives? (See pp. 32–33.)

3 **Read verse 2.** How does John further explain how God in Christ has dealt with our sin? (See pp. 33–36.)

4 **Read verses 3–6.** Why does John focus on obedience to Christ's commands as a characteristic of the true Christian? How would you answer the charge that this smacks of legalism rather than of love? (See pp. 36–38.)

(Q) 1 John 2:7–14
5. How the true light shines (pp. 39–45)

5 **Read verses 7–8.** How should we understand this 'command' that is 'old' yet 'new'? (See pp. 39–40.)

6 **Read verses 9–11.** 'Light and love go together.' Why does John emphasize this link so strongly? How do his words challenge us? (See pp. 41–42.)

7 **Read verses 12–14.** Who are the 'dear children', 'fathers' and 'young men' of this poetic section? What particular convictions does John want each group to hold, and why? (See pp. 42–45.)

SESSION FOUR

(Q) 1 John 2:15–17
6. What's wrong with the world? (pp. 46–52)

1 What does John mean by 'the world'? (See pp. 46–47.)

2 How does 'the world' attract and tempt us? Why does David Jackman describe this as a 'deceptive attraction'? (See pp. 47–51.)

3 What does it mean to do 'the will of God', and what is the outcome of adopting this as the guiding principle of our lives? (See pp. 51–52.)

ⓠ 1 John 2:18–23
7. Realism about the enemy (pp. 53–58)

4 'It doesn't really matter what you believe so long as you believe it sincerely.' Why is it important not just to be sincere but to 'know the truth' (verses 20–21)? (See pp. 53–54.)

5 What is an 'antichrist'? By what two tests may we recognize antichrists? (See pp. 54–56.) What antichrist movements do we come up against today?

6 How can we counteract their activity and influence? (See pp. 56–58.)

ⓠ 1 John 2:24–29
8. Staying on course as a Christian (pp. 59–64)

7 Surrounded as we are by pressures to stray (verse 26), John points us to three strategies to ensure that we 'continue in' Christ (verse 28). The first comes in verses 24–25. Why is it important to see that the great truths of the Christian faith 'remain' in us? (See pp. 59–61.)

8 **Read verses 26–27.** 'Let God's anointing teach you' (the second strategy). What does John mean? How does this teaching keep us from being led 'astray'? (See pp. 61–62.)

9 **Read verses 28–29.** John's third exhortation is to 'continue in' Christ, which is evidenced by doing 'what is right'. How does the 'vine' imagery in John 15 illuminate these verses? (See pp. 62–64.)

SESSION FIVE

ⓠ 1 John 3:1–6
9. Living in God's family (pp. 65–73)

1 **Read verses 1–2.** 'Behold, what manner of love the Father hath bestowed upon us' (AV). What 'manner of love' is this? What has it accomplished for us? What will be the ultimate outcome of this love relationship? (See pp. 65–70.)

2 **Read verse 3.** What does it mean to 'purify ourselves'? What is our motivation in this? (See pp. 70–71.)

3 **Read verses 4–6.** How does John define sin? How did Jesus' 'appearance' take away our sins? What is the evidence, in our own lives, that sin has been dealt with? (See pp. 71–73.)

Q 1 John 3:7–10
10. Be what you are (pp. 74–80)

4 **Read verses 7–8a.** Why did John need to point out to his readers that the 'one who does what is right is righteous'? Why do we, too, need that reminder in order not to be led astray? (See pp. 75–76.)

5 **Read verses 8b–10.**

    a. How did Jesus 'destroy the devil's work'? 'Why then,' asks David Jackman, 'do we see the devil still at work today?' (See pp. 77–78.)

    b. 'What are we to do about the devil's continuing activity in our own lives?' What does John mean when he says that a Christian 'cannot go on sinning'? (See pp. 78–80.)

SESSION SIX

Q 1 John 3:11–18
11. A faith that is real (pp. 81–85)

1 John continues to contrast the children of God and the children of the devil. What are the 'two basic attitudes' that enable us to distinguish between them? (See pp. 81–83.)

2 What is the big contrast between Cain and Jesus that John focuses on? How does Jesus' example motivate us to love 'with actions and in truth'? (See pp. 83–85.)

Q 1 John 3:19–24
12. How to please God (pp. 86–91)

3 **Read verses 19–22a.** Why do we sometimes doubt whether we have got anywhere in the Christian life? How in fact can we 'have confidence before God'? (See pp. 86–88.)

4 **Read verses 22b–24.**

    a. What makes this promise about receiving 'anything we ask' from God so difficult for us? (See p. 88.)

    b. What does the obedience of which John speaks consist of? What is the role of the Spirit in this? (See pp. 89–91.)

1 John 4:1–6
13. Testing the spirits (pp. 92–97)

5 **Read verses 1–3.**

   a. Why does John's mention of the Spirit at the end of chapter 3 prompt him to remind his readers to 'test the spirits'? Why do we need to do so too? (See pp. 92–93.)

   b. How can we distinguish between spirits from God and spirits of antichrist? (See pp. 93–95.)

6 **Read verses 4–6.**

   a. How can John say that the believers 'have overcome' the false prophets, even though they are still around? (See pp. 95–96.)

   b. What is attractive, yet false, about the 'viewpoint of the world'? (See pp. 96–97.)

SESSION SEVEN

1 John 4:7–12
14. Does God really love us? (pp. 98–104)

1 **Read verses 7–8.** 'God is love.' Spend some time exploring the depths of this, 'one of the most profound statements of the whole Bible'. How does God's love empower us to love? (See pp. 98–100.)

2 **Read verses 9–10.** What do Jesus' coming and death teach us about the quality of this love of God? (See pp. 100–102.)

3 **Read verses 11–12.** What is the clear implication of the fact that 'God so loved us'? Francis Schaeffer described Christian love as 'the ultimate apologetic': what did he mean? (See pp. 102–104.)

1 John 4:13–21
15. Grounds of assurance (pp. 105–112)

4 Because Christians do sometimes doubt the reality of their faith, John gives his readers five pieces of evidence. The first is in verse 13. How can we know that we have received the Spirit, and hence that 'we live in [God] and he in us'? (See pp. 105–107.)

5 **Read verse 14** for the second piece of evidence. How does the apostles' testimony help us to be sure of Christian truth today? (See pp. 107–108.)

6 **Read verse 15.** What does John mean by the word 'acknowledge', and how does this verse provide us with a third basis of assurance? (See pp. 108–109.)

7 Our fourth piece of evidence is the experience of a love relationship with God (read verses 16–19). How does this give us 'confidence on the day of judgment'? (See pp. 109–111.)

8 **Read verses 20–21**, where John returns to the theme of love for our fellow Christians. How do these verses provide us with both our fifth piece of evidence and a challenge? (See p. 112.)

SESSION EIGHT

(Q) 1 John 5:1–5
16. Faith – the key to victory (pp. 113–124)

1 Continuing with his theme of love, John begins to weave in another – 'faith'. What is the difference between the vague idea of 'faith' that many people have, and 'faith' according to this and other passages in the New Testament? (See pp. 113–117.)

2 John writes of three ways in which faith is shown to be genuine in a Christian's life. The first turns the focus back on love. How does love relate to, and demonstrate, faith? (See pp. 118–119, and look back to pp. 113–114.)

3 John's second proof of genuine faith is obedience. How do faith, love and obedience belong together? (See pp. 119–121.)

4 John's third evidence of true faith is victory. What does he mean when he says that Christians 'overcome the world'? Such talk may not seem realistic as we look at the world around us – but how can we be sure that it is in fact 'the only ultimate realism'? (See pp. 121–124.)

(Q) 1 John 5:6–12
17. Evidence – the key to faith (pp. 125–134)

5 **Read verses 6–9.** To understand this rather puzzling passage we need to remind ourselves of the religious context into which John was writing (see pp. 125–126).

a. In what sense did Jesus 'come by water'? (See p. 127.)

b. Why does John stress that Jesus 'did not come by water only, but by water and blood'? What does blood signify here? (See p. 127.)

c. In what sense does 'the Spirit' also testify about Jesus? (See pp. 127–130.)

6 **Read verses 10–12.**

a. The Christian believer, too, has the same 'testimony in himself' (RSV). What is the objective basis of this subjective dimension? (See pp. 130–132.)

b. This testimony is described as 'eternal life'. What is this 'life' which God has given us? (See pp. 132–134.)

SESSION NINE

(Q) **1 John 5:13–21**
18. You can be sure (pp. 135–149)

1 **Read verse 13.** In the last session we looked at what it means to have eternal life. Why is John anxious that his readers may 'know' that they have this life? (See pp. 135–137.)

2 One aspect of this 'knowing' is confidence in prayer.

a. **Read verses 14–15.** Why can we be confident, or bold, in prayer? About what sort of prayer (and that only) can we be confident? (See pp. 137–140.)

b. **Read verses 16–17.** We are to pray for fellow Christians who fall into 'a sin that does not lead to death', but 'there is a sin that leads to death'. What explanations of these difficult verses have been offered? What do you think John is saying? (See pp. 140–144.)

3 **Read verse 18.** Here is something else that Christians 'know': that true Christians do not go on sinning. Who is the 'One who was born of God' who keeps us safe under attack from the devil? (See pp. 144–146.)

4 **Read verse 19.** Think of some of the many ways in which we see that the 'world' is clearly 'under the control of the evil one'. Christians 'know' that they are under a different lordship. What are some implications of this? (See pp. 146–148.)

5 **Read verse 20.** The last great certainty to which John directs our attention is the foundation of all the others. To what different facets of knowing Jesus does he point? (See pp. 148–149.)

6 **Read verse 21.** Why is this warning still appropriate to us today? Think about factors in your own life which might be in danger of squeezing God out of the central position. (See p. 149.)

7 At the beginning of our study of 1 John, we saw that David Jackman compared its structure to a spiral staircase. 'The view gets more wonderful as you climb' (p. 8). As you have 'climbed', what wonderful things have come into your own personal 'view'?

SESSION TEN

2 John
19. Priorities of truth and love (pp. 150–164)

1 **Read verses 1–3.**
   a. Who do you think are 'the elder' and the 'lady chosen by God'? (See pp. 151–152.)
   b. Explore John's use of the terms 'truth', 'grace', 'mercy', 'peace' and 'love' in these verses. (See pp. 152–153.)

2 **Read verses 4–6.** What does it mean to walk 'in the truth', 'in obedience' and in 'love'? How are the three intertwined? How can we encourage ourselves and each other in this walk? (See pp. 153–156.)

3 **Read verses 7–11.**
   a. How does John help his readers to recognize and resist false teaching? What does it mean (and not mean!) to 'continue in the teaching of Christ'? (See pp. 156–160.)
   b. Having written so much about love, why does John now tell his readers to take the apparently unloving course of not welcoming false teachers into their homes? How can we apply this to our own encounters with people who teach error? (See pp. 160–163.)

4 **Read verses 12–13.** What do these verses tell us about the relationship between John and the church to which he was writing, and between local churches? (See pp. 163–164.)

SESSION ELEVEN

ⓠ 3 John
20. Learning by example (pp. 165–177)

1 What do we know about the background to this, John's 'most personal' letter? (See p. 165.)

2 **Read verses 1–8.**

   a. What do we know about Gaius? What does the relationship between Gaius and John teach us about Christian friendship? (See p. 166.)

   b. How does John's prayer for Gaius's physical health help us to correct some misconceptions about the body which have crept into the church from time to time? (See pp. 167–168.)

   c. John twice mentions Gaius's faithfulness. In what respects, in particular, was he faithful? (See pp. 168–169.)

   d. Who were the 'brothers and sisters' who were 'strangers', to whom Gaius was encouraged to 'show hospitality'? (See p. 169.)

   e. What do verses 7 and 8 tell us about the motivation for Christian service, and about relationships between Christian workers and supporters? (See pp. 169–171.)

3 **Read verses 9–10.** What do we know about Diotrephes? Where, fundamentally, had he gone wrong? (See pp. 171–174.)

4 **Read verses 11–12.**

   a. John's condemnation of Diotrephes leads him to urge Gaius not to 'imitate what is evil'. Since no-one has seen God, what does John mean when he says that those who do evil have 'not seen God'? (See pp. 174–175.)

   b. By contrast, Demetrius was universally recognized for his goodness. What do we know about him? (See pp. 175–176.)

5 **Read verses 13–15.** 'Peace to you' was a conventional way of closing a letter, but what significance does the greeting assume here? (See pp. 176–177.)

6 In what ways have the varied examples of Gaius, Diotrephes and Demetrius challenged you personally?

The Bible Speaks Today: Old Testament series

The Message of Genesis 1 – 11
The dawn of creation
David Atkinson

The Message of Genesis 12 – 50
From Abraham to Joseph
Joyce G. Baldwin

The Message of Exodus
The days of our pilgrimage
Alec Motyer

The Message of Leviticus
Free to be holy
Derek Tidball

The Message of Numbers
Journey to the promised land
Raymond Brown

The Message of Deuteronomy
Not by bread alone
Raymond Brown

The Message of Joshua
Promise and people
David G. Firth

The Message of Judges
Grace abounding
Michael Wilcock

The Message of Ruth
The wings of refuge
David Atkinson

The Message of Samuel
Personalities, potential, politics and power
Mary J. Evans

The Message of Kings
God is present
John W. Olley

The Message of Chronicles
One church, one faith, one Lord
Michael Wilcock

The Message of Ezra and Haggai
Building for God
Robert Fyall

The Message of Nehemiah
God's servant in a time of change
Raymond Brown

The Message of Esther
God present but unseen
David G. Firth

The Message of Job
Suffering and grace
David Atkinson

The Bible Speaks Today: New Testament series

The Message of Matthew
The kingdom of heaven
Michael Green

The Message of Mark
The mystery of faith
Donald English

The Message of Luke
The Saviour of the world
Michael Wilcock

The Message of John
Here is your King!
Bruce Milne

**The Message of the Sermon
on the Mount (Matthew 5 – 7)**
Christian counter-culture
John Stott

The Message of Acts
To the ends of the earth
John Stott

The Message of Romans
God's good news for the world
John Stott

The Message of 1 Corinthians
Life in the local church
David Prior

The Message of 2 Corinthians
Power in weakness
Paul Barnett

The Message of Galatians
Only one way
John Stott

The Message of Ephesians
God's new society
John Stott

The Message of Philippians
Jesus our joy
Alec Motyer

**The Message of Colossians and
Philemon**
Fullness and freedom
Dick Lucas

**The Message of
1 and 2 Thessalonians**
Preparing for the coming King
John Stott

The Bible Speaks Today:
Bible Themes series

The Message of the Living God
His glory, his people, his world
Peter Lewis

The Message of the Resurrection
Christ is risen!
Paul Beasley-Murray

The Message of the Cross
Wisdom unsearchable, love indestructible
Derek Tidball

The Message of Salvation
By God's grace, for God's glory
Philip Graham Ryken

The Message of Creation
Encountering the Lord of the universe
David Wilkinson

The Message of Heaven and Hell
Grace and destiny
Bruce Milne

The Message of Mission
The glory of Christ in all time and space
Howard Peskett and Vinoth Ramachandra

The Message of Prayer
Approaching the throne of grace
Tim Chester

The Message of the Trinity
Life in God
Brian Edgar

The Message of Evil and Suffering
Light into darkness
Peter Hicks

The Message of the Holy Spirit
The Spirit of encounter
Keith Warrington

The Message of Holiness
Restoring God's masterpiece
Derek Tidball

The Message of Sonship
At home in God's household
Trevor Burke

The Message of the Word of God
The glory of God made known
Tim Meadowcroft

The Message of Women
Creation, grace and gender
Derek and Dianne Tidball

The Message of the Church
Assemble the people before me
Chris Green

The Message of the Person of Christ
The Word made flesh
Robert Letham

The Message of Worship
Celebrating the glory of God in the whole of life
John Risbridger

The Message of Spiritual Warfare
The Lord is a warrior; the Lord is his name
Keith Ferdinando

The Message of Discipleship
Authentic followers of Jesus in today's world
Peter Morden

The Message of Love
The only thing that counts
Patrick Mitchel

The Message of Wisdom
Learning and living the way of the Lord
Daniel J. Estes